HOW TO MAKE YOUR SCRIPT BETTER THAN THE REST

Tips and Tricks for
Writing and Revising Screenplays

by Kathy McCullough

D0920695

Kathy McCullough Books
Los Angeles

How to Make Your Script Better Than the Rest:
Tips and Tricks for Writing and Revising Screenplays

Copyright © 2021 by Kathy McCullough

All Rights Reserved.

ISBN: 978-0-578-87065-6 (trade paperback)
Library of Congress Control Number: 2021904403

www.kathymcculloughbooks.com

TABLE OF CONTENTS

FADE IN:

PROLOGUE

Before I became a full-time writer, I worked for many years as a story analyst (also known as a "script reader"). It's a popular job for aspiring screenwriters and a useful one, because it's like taking a screenwriting class every day. The reader's job is to figure out what's working in a script and, more importantly, what *isn't* working and why. Having to study other writers' scripts daily helped me to identify problems in my own work that I might never have recognized otherwise. After reading and analyzing thousands of scripts during my time as a story analyst, for dozens of different companies, from Imagine Films and Castle Rock Entertainment to Participant Media and HBO, I became increasingly better at identifying common problems in screenplays of all genres, and at finding solutions for those problems. This led to my writing a regular column on the craft, called "Script Buzz," which I sent out as an e-newsletter and which appeared on the website for the Script Nannies, a script consulting company I ran for several years with fellow story analyst Joanne Lammers. Most of the essays in this book are based on those columns and have been revised and updated for this book. A few additional essays were first published on online writing websites or in print. There are also two new essays, inspired by screenwriting classes I've taught.

Because the bulk of the essays address problems I found in scripts when I was a reader, this is less of a "**How to Write...**" book than a "**How to Fix...**" or "**How to Improve....**" one. In other words, the essays are designed to help you take the script you're already working on and make it better, and make you a better writer in the process. The advice combines the basic with the advanced, but whatever stage you're in in your writing process or career, my hope is that by applying these tips you'll raise the level of your craft and write screenplays that stand out.

Feel free to skip around within the book in order to focus on the issues you're most interested in, or areas you're having problems with at the moment. Certain problems may be addressed in more than one essay. This is because these issues tend to come up more often than others in scripts that are submitted to production companies, and also because they're key to a great screenplay and therefore ones you should definitely pay attention to.

The movies referenced in the essays dealing with craft (plot, characterization, structure) are either classic films, or those I consider modern classics, and/or films that were critically praised for their screenplays. A list of all the films mentioned in the book can be found in the Appendix. They're all worth watching and studying. If there are any you haven't already seen, I recommend streaming them or borrowing the DVD from your local library.

Unless I'm referencing a specific character in a film, I've chosen to use the neutral "they" pronoun in the essays.

I. <u>NUTS AND BOLTS</u>

The following chapters discuss minor craft issues. You don't need to obsess over these issues until well into the revision process, but I decided to put this section first, because they address many of the first questions I'm asked by beginning screenwriters and students in the classes I've taught. These essays are also worth glancing at before you start a script, because applying these tips early on will save you time revising later.

FAQs
WHITE SPACE: WHAT SHOULD APPEAR ON THE PAGE
CHARACTER BYTES
DESCRIPTION
DON'T BE VAGUE

FAQs

FAQs often come at the end of books, but since I always end up getting asked many of these questions on Day 1 of any screenwriting class, I've decided to include them first. In addition to topics I'm often asked by new writers, there are also solutions here to common problems I see in beginning scripts. Follow these tips to make your script look polished and professional.

Formatting: Most screenplays are written in the Courier Font, 12 point. There's generally a one-inch margin at the sides and at the top and bottom. Resist shrinking your type size or pushing your text beyond these margins in order to reduce your page count. (Spec scripts are generally about 105 to 115 pages.) A better solution is to carefully go through your script and cut down description, repetition, and long dialogue chunks. Don't number the scenes (which is only necessary for shooting scripts).

Software: Presently, Final Draft is the most common screenwriting program used in Hollywood, but it's not necessary for you to have this program to write your script. There are plenty of other screenwriting templates and software. Scripts are submitted electronically via pdf, so as long as you're able to save your document as a pdf and it's properly formatted, you'll be fine. That said, Final Draft is easy to use and does a great job at formatting. If you can afford it, or can get a student discount, it's worth having.

V.O./O.C./O.S.: O.C. (off-camera) and O.S. (off-screen) are interchangeable, although O.C. is more commonly see in teleplays, while O.S. is used in screenplays. O.S. means the character speaking is literally off-screen. They could be in the next room, or we could be hearing dialogue from a preceding or following scene bleeding over. In all cases, the dialogue is going on in the story in the present. V.O. (voice-over) is narration spoken by a character not currently in the action, such as someone telling a story or reflecting on their past.

Subtitles, foreign words: Highlight foreign words in dialogue by putting them in *italics*. If you're translating them as well, put the English text in parentheses or brackets below the foreign text. If you're not fluent in the language, stick to English and put "in Italian" (without the quotes) in the parenthetical under the character's name.

Sluglines: Sluglines should begin with EXT. or INT., followed by the location, then a dash, and then the time of day. Although many writers tend to be casual about the sluglines, the more exact you are, the less likely you'll confuse the reader. Use CONTINUOUS for the time of day only when a character is moving directly from one location to another, such as from the bathroom to the bedroom. If the scene is simply the next one in the story, then put the time of day. SAME can be used for intercut scenes, such as telephone conversations (see below for more on this). LATER is used when the next scene is the same location as the previous one but at a later period of time.

On-screen text: Titles such as ENGLAND, 1942 or FIVE YEARS LATER simply need to be put on their own description line. There is no need to write out SUBTITLE as well. However, the line will stand out more if you underline it and/or put it in bold type. If you want to indicate different periods of time without subtitles (such as when cutting back and forth between two periods) then put the date at the end of the slugline.

Phone conversations: For phone conversations in which we see both parties, first establish one location with a slugline, a couple of lines of description, and dialogue. Then, on a separate line, write:

INTERCUT WITH:

You can then establish the second location with a slugline, description, and dialogue. For the rest of the scene, you only need dialogue and description, because we'll know the conversation is cutting between the two locations.

How specific should you be?: The more detailed you are in your screenplay, the more authentic the script will be for the reader, but you don't want to go overboard. Below are some guidelines for specific elements:

Characters: Distinguish characters via their manner, attitude, posture and behavior rather than physical characteristics. While an age range is helpful, avoid writing out specific physical traits such as height, weight, skin color, hair color, etc. unless these details are essential to the plot.

Location: "A typical suburb," or "generic city" aren't particularly vivid setting descriptions and aren't likely to bring the location to life for the reader. If your location is a fictional small town, provide any necessary details, including its name, that will help make the town come alive. If you're setting your movie in a real location, like Chicago for instance, then bring Chicago to life for us by emphasizing the areas and qualities of the city that make it unique. (More on this subject in "Don't Be Vague.")

Camera directions: In the early decades of Hollywood scriptwriting, camera directions were often included in a script, but they're now frowned on unless the writer is also directing. The cleaner the page, the more impact the action and dialogue will have and the faster the script will read. You can imply camera directions, however, by wording the description carefully. For instance, instead of inserting "POV Danny's phone: the time reads 12:15 p.m." you can just write, "Danny checks his phone. It's 12:15."

Songs: Just as the director decides where the camera should go, the job of picking songs for your movie generally belongs to the music supervisor. Include a specific song only if it relates directly to the action of your story— but be aware that the song may be changed in the film, depending on rights availability and the artistic choices of others working on the film.

Parentheticals: Indented parentheses under the character's name, above the dialogue, are used to indicate a character's tone of voice, or an action (or, as discussed above, to indicate a language other than English). However, this device is often overused. As much as possible, let the actor determine how to interpret the tone. If you're using the parenthetical for an action, keep it brief. If the action goes over a short sentence, put it on a description line.

Some of these points may seem petty, but they can have a cumulative effect on the reader. The slicker and more professional your script, the less likely the reader will be taken out of your story, and the more likely you are to get a positive response.

WHITE SPACE: WHAT SHOULD APPEAR ON THE PAGE

Producers and readers often talk about "white space" when they discuss the look of a screenplay. The goal of the writer should be to find just the right balance of text to blank space. But what is the right amount? Is it better to have no description than too much?

One script page is considered to be one minute of film, and this is worth keeping in mind as you write, but the issue of white space isn't always this simple. Battle scenes, for instance, can be described in one or two paragraphs, but may take up ten or twenty minutes of film time, while a two-page dialogue-only scene may take less than a minute. On average, however, this "page a minute" rule holds true. This means, in general, that if your script is 80 pages long, it might be too short; if it's 180 pages, it's too long. Unless it's an historical epic, keep the script under 120 pages. As mentioned above, spec scripts tend to be 105 to 115 pages on average. So what should appear on those 110 pages?

Consider first of all what type of script you're writing. For comedies, small character pieces, and thrillers, less is always more. The pacing of these films is key to their success, so you don't want your reader getting bogged down in long setting descriptions or overly detailed action. However, you also don't want a script that contains nothing but dialogue. Dialogue with no description comes across as "talking heads," making your story seem stagnant, stagy, and more suited to a television soap opera than a cinematic feature. If you have two characters talking, make sure you get across exactly what we are *seeing* on the screen. What are the characters doing? Where are they in the space? Ideally, they're engaging in an activity that either underscores or ironically contradicts the dialogue. This doesn't mean that you have to write out every beat of a character folding laundry for instance.

"Sasha folds laundry" is enough, but if she *is* folding laundry, how does this action support the dramatic intent of the scene? Perhaps she slaps Dave with a towel flirtatiously at one point, or dumps freshly cleaned and folded sheets on the floor in a moment of anger.

Even if you're writing an epic or historical drama, this doesn't give you carte blanche to fill the page with description. Include only the resonant details and only those that clearly move the action forward. If you're writing a battle scene or a chase sequence, and you can cut something out without affecting the overall understanding of how the action plays out, then delete it. Also, make sure your description doesn't take up more than five or six lines on the page. If it does, break it up into shorter paragraphs, thereby adding that coveted white space.

A few things to avoid in any genre: a detailed physical description of a character; every beat of a simple activity; actions that are assumed (if a character gets out of the car, we can assume they closes the car door behind them); the internal thoughts of a character or background information it's not possible to show on the screen; overly detailed descriptions of any setting; a summary of an emotional response, such as "Ella gets angry." Show this instead, either with the character's dialogue or by a specific action the character commits.

Be aware that producers, agents, studio executives, and readers tend to skim the description, so the less you have of it, the more they are likely to catch it all. That's why your description needs to be succinct and sharp. Long speeches will also be glossed over. As with description, avoid having dialogue of more than four or five lines. Occasionally, characters do make speeches that are longer than five lines, but the key word here is "occasionally," and the speech better be gripping and essential to the story. Otherwise, pare your dialogue down to its essence. It's usually either the middle line or the last line of a dialogue patch that contains the gist of what the character is saying.

Reading produced screenplays will help you get a better sense of what to include and what to avoid in both dialogue and description. Read as many scripts as you can, in all genres. (Scripts of produced films are easy to find online via a simple search.) Different professional screenwriters often have different styles. For instance, some are a little more descriptive. This tends to be true of screenwriters who began as novelists. However, their prose is usually so superior they can get away with this—but this doesn't mean that busy executives will actually read it all. Writer-directors tend to be sparer, because they know in their head what they want to see on the screen and therefore don't feel the need to spell it all out. As you read more scripts, you'll be able to identify what works and why. For instance, a clever bit of description in a comedy will help convey the lightweight tone of the piece quickly, while a terse, tightly-paced action sequence will create suspense. Aim to emulate this ability to evoke in your readers the same emotional response they'd have watching the actual movie.

CHARACTER BYTES

In addition to avoiding too much physical detail in your character descriptions (discussed in the essays above), there are other minor elements of characterization you should pay attention to when crafting your script. More complex character development issues will be discussed in later chapters, but for this chapter we'll deal with the tiny technical details that writers often overlook.

Here are a few:

Introductions: As mentioned above, resist being too specific in the physical description of your character, unless something about their physical appearance is central to the plot. However, you don't want to give us just their name and age range. We need to know *why* this character is special. This doesn't mean you should include long detailed paragraphs describing the character's background, fears, and hopes, etc. Such passages are appropriate for novels, but film is a visual medium, and therefore you need to bring your character to life *in action*. Show their unique personality in the way they respond to the world around them in the opening scenes. What your character says and does will have more impact than what you say about them.

Beware of casting your movie in advance. Picturing a well-known actor such as Charlize Theron as your lead can help you bring your character to life in your head. However, don't include "Charlize Theron -type" or "Think Charlize Theron" in the description. This marks you as an amateur, not to mention the fact that it will turn off any actor who *isn't* Charlize Theron. Also, avoid copying or even emulating behavioral or speech gimmicks from characters in other movies. Your script will end up coming across as derivative rather than fresh.

"One-string" or "prop" characters: "One-string" characters are supporting figures who have minor roles that are threaded through the story. They may be in only a few scenes, but they play at least a small role in advancing the action or conflict. A landlady who's in a number of scenes in which she interacts with the leads will be more memorable if she has a name and a specific personality (grumpy, nosey, etc.). However, a "prop" character, such as a store clerk or a mail carrier who is only present in one or two brief scenes and never seen or mentioned again, should be identified as "clerk" or "mail carrier" because giving them names and too detailed of a description will confuse a reader into thinking they're more important to the story than they are. You can still give even these prop characters flair and color via their distinct behavior and dialogue, however. Always try to give an actor, even one who appears in only one scene, something interesting to play. Your script will be much richer as a result – just be careful that a minor player doesn't end up more interesting than your leads. (More on one-string characters in "Supporting Characters: The Cornerstone of Your Script.")

Similar Character Names: Production executives and story analysts read scripts fast, so you want to do everything you can to avoid confusion in your writing. One of the most common confusion points is using characters with similar names. For example, a script in which all the characters' names begin with M (Margaret, Mark, Mike, Martha, Mary and Matt) is the writing equivalent of casting the movie with a roster of actors who all look alike. This makes it difficult, especially at the beginning of the story, to remember who is who. In order not to break the flow of your story, make the characters names as distinct from one another as possible. Don't have any that share the first letter. Don't have any that rhyme (Stacy, Tracy) or that are even close in sound (Darcy, Marla). Coming up with distinct character names is just one more way you help make the characters themselves distinct and diverse.

Capitalization: It's standard practice in screenplays to put the name of the character in all caps when we first meet them. Although this was originally for production purposes, it helps with reading as well, because it makes it easy to spot the entrance of a new character. For this reason, it's confusing when character names are capitalized throughout the script or capitalized erratically. Again, the reader must slow down and think: is this a new character? However, don't capitalize the names when they're first spoken in dialogue; only capitalize their entrance in the description.
(Note: In teleplays for multi-camera sitcoms, character names *are* capitalized in all of the description.)

Using more than one name: If a character's name is FRANK MATTHEWS, refer to him as Frank OR Matthews after introducing him. If "FRANK" is used as a dialogue heading, but "Matthews" is used in the description, this will be confusing. However, in the dialogue, other characters may refer to him as either Frank or Matthews, or by a nickname. Description is formal; dialogue is informal. If a character's name is Frank Matthews but he's posing as a man named John Walker, again you want to pick one of the names and stick with it. If we meet him first as Frank, then keep him as Frank in the description and dialogue heading, even when he's using his fake name. If we meet him first as John and his real name isn't revealed until the end, as a surprise, then stick with John. If the character actually transforms, then it's acceptable to use another name for the alternate personality, because this will help the reader visualize and keep track of the change. For instance, in THE AVENGERS, when Dr. Banner becomes the

Hulk, he's then referred to as the Hulk. Similarly, Bruce Wayne becomes Batman in THE DARK NIGHT in both the description and dialogue heading.

Adhering to these guidelines will result in a clearer, cleaner script, which will allow your story to shine through and hold a reader's attention from beginning to end.

DESCRIPTION

Description may seem to be the least important part of your screenplay, yet scripts are read before they are filmed, and therefore well-written description is nearly as important in a screenplay as it is in a novel. Here are some dos and don'ts to consider as you fine-tune your description. Some of these were touched on in the essays above, but they're important enough to repeat:

Do keep it short. Long passages of text will slow the pace of your script and annoy busy executives and readers, who will likely skim the same sentences you've spent so much time laboring over. It's not necessary to describe locations, characters, or objects in minute detail. For characters, for example, it's enough to provide the gender, age range, and one or two effective adjectives or phrases in order to give us an idea of who this person is and why we should be interested in them. Physical traits aren't necessary unless they're integral to the story. There's a practical side to this sparseness in character description: you want to make the role appealing to as wide a range of actors as possible. Similarly, with settings, it's enough to say that a room is messy and give a couple of key examples, and let the set decorator flesh it out in production. There's no need to mention every pile of old magazines, crushed soda cans, and dirty ashtrays.

Do add white space. As discussed in the "White Space" essay above, if you have a descriptive passage that is necessarily long, like a battle scene, then break up the action into several paragraphs, none more than five or six lines in length. This will make the description easier to read and will create a sense of forward momentum. However, even in action scenes, there's no need to spell out every beat. By the time the movie is made, a host of technicians and artists will have joined together to choreograph any complicated visual sequence.

Don't include camera directions. You may occasionally see camera directions in scripts by produced writers, but the practice is considered out of style now. Your goal is to write a script that involves the reader completely in your story, and constantly cutting away from the action to give us a new camera angle interrupts the flow and ironically makes the script feel less like a real movie experience.

Do break up sentences into shots. As mentioned in "FAQs," you can *imply* camera directions via separate sentences. For example, "Chuck turns over the envelope. His name is scrawled on the front." The second sentence indicates a close-up on the envelope without the writer having to write out "CLOSE-UP." Any change of angle or point of view should be indicated by a new sentence. "Hector slides into a booth, while across the room Sophie glances up and sees him" is not as cinematic as "Hector slides into a booth. Across the room, Sophie glances up and sees him." The latter works better in a screenplay, because the two sentences mimic the change in focal point and therefore imply a new shot.

Do be expressive. Just because your description is short doesn't mean it has to be dull. Whenever possible choose dynamic verbs and clever adjectives. Instead having someone walk across the room, have them march, stomp, trudge, dash, or stumble, depending on what's appropriate for the scene. You want to bring the picture to life for the reader, and a few well-chosen words will do this for you.

Do try to emulate the tone of your script in the description. Description for a comedy should be wry and snappy. Description for a thriller should be tense and foreboding. Read produced scripts in different genres to see examples of how other writers have achieved this.

Don't use the passive voice. For instance, "Dave is hit by a falling brick" is less dynamic than "A brick falls and hits Dave." The latter comes across as closer to real time. This is also true of sentences like "Sheryl is rushing across the room when she's intercepted by Deanna" as opposed to "Sheryl rushes across the room. Deanna intercepts her." The second version makes the action feel more immediate and therefore a better translation of what we see on screen. Similarly, eliminate phrases like "starts to" or "begins to." "Kyle starts to sit down" has less energy than "Kyle sits."

Don't include internal thoughts or feelings. It's fine to throw in an occasional reference to how a character is feeling (angry, annoyed), although it's always better if you can *show* the emotion via action. However, always avoid detailed mental processes: "Phoebe snatches up the knife, remembering how Joe had belittled her at dinner." Put in the description *only* what we can actually see on the screen, and let the reader figure out the rest—just as the audience will when they see the movie. If we can't see it on screen, leave it out.

Don't talk to the reader. There are a few professional writers who are known for throwing jokes and asides into their description, but they've succeeded *in spite* of this, not because of it. Again, as mentioned above, you don't want to do anything that will break the reader's concentration and take them out of the story. Corny or snide commentary points up the artificiality of the world you're trying to persuade the reader to believe in. The exception is when you're trying to establish tone. In comedies especially, writers may toss in a bit of witty commentary here and there. This has to be done exceptionally well, however, and sparingly. Otherwise, it will detract from your story rather than enhance it.

As suggested above, the best way to learn what kind of description works well is to read scripts by produced writers. Note when a writer's description grabs you, and, just as importantly, notice when it bores you. The more you read—and write—the better your description will be and the more likely executives and readers will savor and appreciate it, rather than skip it.

DON'T BE VAGUE

If you want the producer, agent or story analyst reading your screenplay to be completely engaged by the world you've created, it's important you be as specific as possible in bringing your tale to life. The vaguer and blander your writing, the harder it is for a reader to visualize and become emotionally involved in what they are reading. This may seem to contradict much of the advice given in the essays above. However, avoiding vagueness doesn't mean you need to include chunks of description or add minute physical descriptions of your characters. Not being vague means making it very clear who your characters are, where the story is taking place, and what exactly is happening in each scene.

Characters: As I've mentioned in earlier essays, it's not necessary for you to describe your characters down to their shoe size. Unless it's essential to the plot, there's no reason to specify hair color, or whether or not a character is short or tall. However, an age range, such as "JERMAINE (40s)" for instance, gives us a general idea of where this character is in their life. For any character under 20, give the exact age. A child who is nine is lot different from a child who is eleven. It also helps to have one or two concrete personality traits for your principal characters. If you can show this in action, great, but it's acceptable to do a little more "telling" in this case, as long as you keep it brief. For instance, you might include a line after your character is introduced telling us that they are "organized to the point of obsession" or "unrelentingly cheerful." The best introductory descriptions foreshadow conflict, because we know this trait will be challenged somehow, and they also make the character someone we want to know more about. While we don't need to know every beat of the character's backstory, it's essential to place your character in a dramatic, emotional, and physical context as the story unfolds. In other words, if your character is an adult and employed, then we need to know what their profession is fairly early on. If they're out of work, make this clear and show us why and what this means for them financially and personally. The character's relationships with those around them are also important. The script may be a romantic comedy and focus mainly on the protagonist's relationship with the love interest, but in the real world, they will also have friends, colleagues, and family. Including a few of these relationships in your story will give the plot more texture and help flesh out the leads as we see how they interact with the other people in their life. (There are, of course, exceptions to this, such as films that intentionally only have one or two characters in them, such as BEFORE SUNRISE and its sequels.)

Dialogue: Avoid having characters speak in generalities or talk in a circular manner. While you want to avoid being on-the-nose, if you're too ambiguous, it will be impossible to tell what you're trying to get across in the dialogue. If a character is purposely trying to avoid answering a question or addressing a difficult issue, make sure that what they *are* saying is specific, even if it's off point. Comedies especially need strong, clear dialogue. Humor relies on concrete words and images. Ambiguity weakens the joke. Also, make sure each of your characters speaks in a distinct voice. If all of your characters sound the same, they'll blend together and fail to come to life. Think of memorable characters from movies you've seen. Most likely, their unique way of speaking is one of the key traits that helped to define them.

Plot: To keep a reader or viewer engaged in your film story, it's important to be specific about what is happening and why. Movies that fail to explain clearly why an event occurred or why a character has come to a certain conclusion are frustrating for the audience. Also remember that film is a visual medium. When you're writing, visualize what the audience is actually seeing on the screen. Avoid description that tells us what the character is feeling. Instead, show us what they're feeling by describing what they're *doing*.

Setting: Setting is an area that many writers falsely believe *should* be vague. Establishing a specific location, as with describing a character in too much depth, would seem to limit the script's potential, but this is not actually the case. Location is often a character itself in a film, and the more specific you are in describing it, the more it, as well as the events taking place within it and the characters participating in these events, will come to life. Setting your story in Seattle, for example, paints a clearer picture than merely setting it in "a city." Seattle, like most cities, has a particular personality. Include specific characteristics the city is known for, such as its weather and landmarks. If your story has a surreal quality that demands it take place in a fictional urban location, you still need to be specific about what this city looks like, how it is laid out, what type of people live there, etc. Think Gotham in the BATMAN and DARK KNIGHT movies; it may be fictional, but it has a very specific look and feel to it. This is true for suburban and rural settings as well. It's not necessary that a suburb or small town exist on a map, but the town in your story should have a name, even if it's made up, and you should have a clear picture of what it looks like. What's the population? Is the town old or new? What's the ethnic make-up? Is it located in the South? North? Midwest? What's the architecture like? Is it hilly or flat? Not every one of these details needs to be spelled out in the script, but you should be able to answer any of these questions about the town if asked. The more real the location is to the writer, the more believable it will be to the reader. It's true that a location may very well change by the time the movie is made. THE BIG EASY, for example, was originally set in Chicago but ended up taking place in New Orleans. However, both the script and the film used setting as a character. Had the original screenplay taken place in a generic city, it's quite possible it wouldn't have been as compelling to the filmmakers.

Unlike novels, in which every aspect of the story is often brought to life in the text, a screenplay is merely the blueprint for a film—yet scripts are *read* before they're made. The more successful you are in getting your story to come alive for the reader, so that they can "see" what you envision happening on the screen, the better your chances of success. The challenge is to find ways to be concrete and specific while still being brief and keeping the action moving. As always, seek out produced scripts to see how other writers have accomplished this. Vague scripts are forgettable scripts. Vivid screenplays are compelling and memorable.

II. <u>BEFORE YOU BEGIN</u>

Consider this section a "warm-up." These essays are worth reading as part of your screenwriting journey, but some may not apply to where you are in that journey right now. Although the focus of this book, as implied by the title, is to make your script the best it can be, I've added two essays here on finding ideas and getting out the first draft quickly. These essays will be helpful to writers starting out, and they contain advice I've given to students in my screenwriting classes. There are also essays here for writers at any stage on how to develop any ideas you already have into stories that are fresh and original rather than derivative; how to find the inspiration to keep you going; and actions to take when you need a break from writing or aren't quite ready to start.

NEW YEAR'S RESOLUTIONS
HOW TO FIND IDEAS
BEYOND THE PREMISE: HOW TO DEVELOP A COMPELLING STORY
REINVENTING THE WHEEL: HOW TO TRANSCEND A GENRE
JUST WRITE A DRAFT
TWO PEAS IN A POD: AVOIDING CLICHÉS
THEME

NEW YEAR'S SCREENWRITING RESOLUTIONS

Because resolutions can come at any time, I consider "New Year" more metaphorical here than literal (unless you're coincidentally reading this at the end or beginning of a calendar year). Along with your New Year's resolution to finish that script you've been working on, or to start the one you've been thinking about, or to send out the one you've finished, here are some additional goals for any serious writer's list:

1. Take a class, or two. Writing classes offer many benefits. In addition to learning the tools to improve your craft, you'll have access to feedback, both from the instructor and from your peers. A class gives you a set structure, usually with a deadline, to help keep you on track with your writing. A class is also a good place to find people with whom to form a critique group. If you've been writing for a while or have already taken some classes, look for more advanced classes that narrow in on one issue, such as character development or comedy. If your schedule or geographical location prevents you from attending a screenwriting class in person, you can find many classes offered on-line.

2. Don't limit yourself to screenwriting. Learning about or practicing any kind of writing will help you develop your skills. Study plot development and characterization in novels. Study dialogue in plays. Read short stories and graphic novels, many of which contain structures very similar to those of film scripts. Take a fiction or playwriting class.

3. Know the names and works of successful screenwriters. If you don't know who wrote the scripts of the films you most admire, it seems likely you haven't been paying much attention to the screenplays when watching films. Yet, it's hard to imagine any novelist or painter who isn't familiar with the masters who share their calling.

4. Read scripts. You'll see this advice pop up a lot in this book. The more you read other writers' works, the better your own work will be. Reading scripts by writers you admire will allow you to study how they approach different issues, from developing tension to structuring individual scenes. The screenplays of most popular films are easy to find online. Don't limit yourself to produced scripts, however. Reading scripts written by members of your writing group or writing class and providing feedback will help you hone your analytical skills, which you can then use on your own work.

5. Download or purchase the screenplay of a film you admire. Read the script and then watch the movie with the script at hand, noting the differences between the screenplay and the film. Which parts of the script worked on the page but didn't work on the screen—and vice versa? What was cut from the script and why? Sometimes elements such as exposition in dialogue are necessary in a script but not essential in the film, where performance, cinematography, and direction are able to get things across in a more subtle fashion. (A good example is THE GRADUATE, which is a very spare movie yet a fairly dense screenplay.)

6. Watch movies. While it's essential that you study screenplays, you also need to see how the scripts were executed. If you loved the movie, try to pinpoint what it was about the storytelling that made this film excel. If you didn't like the movie, brainstorm a rewrite, fixing the areas you had problems with. Study the films whose scripts you admire and break down the structure. As you watch the films, jot down the scenes in order. Keep a timer or clock nearby and note when the key plot points occur. Afterward, examine your notes to determine how the scenes clump into sequences and acts. It often helps to watch several films in the genre you're writing. When you get stuck, you can consult these breakdowns for help. More advice on watching movies below:

7. <u>Subscribe to a streaming service that has Turner Classic Movies</u>. Because TCM rarely shows any film more than once per month, there's always something different to watch, from classics you've seen several times to rare gems you've never even heard of. At least one award-winning movie is broadcast every day, but even second-rate B-movies are worth a look. In the 1940s and '50s, these movies were cranked out according to established formulas, which makes them very easy to study for structure, pace, and other key plot elements.

8. <u>Watch ten movies known for their superb storytelling</u>. Films that won Oscars for screenwriting or Writers' Guild awards are the obvious choices here, yet there are many movies that were originally overlooked and have gone on to become classics. Films that have been frequently imitated throughout the years (such as SOME LIKE IT HOT and PSYCHO) are also good candidates. Consult the list of movies mentioned in this book, located in the Appendix, for other ideas.

9. <u>Buy or stream your favorite movie, if you don't own it already</u>. Watch the film at least six times in a row. (Yes, you may take bathroom breaks.) After the first three or four times through, you'll cease to be involved in (and therefore distracted by) the story and the mechanics of the film will pop out more clearly. Note how the filmmakers use set design, sound, music, and other elements to foreshadow events. Seek out plants and payoffs in the action and dialogue. Get your hands on the script for the film and study it using the tips discussed earlier in this essay.

10. <u>See at least one movie a week in the theater, if possible.</u> Afterward, analyze what worked in the film and what didn't. Pretend you've been hired to doctor the script, and write out your notes on how to improve the story, character relationships, subplots, etc. Be as detailed as possible.

You can do these tasks any time: before you dive in and begin a script; for guidance or inspiration when you're in the midst of a project; or when you've finished a draft and need a break. These activities will help you refill your creative reserves, so you'll be ready to begin, continue, or begin again with renewed energy and focus.

HOW TO FIND IDEAS

In the classes I've taught, many students arrive with a story they're ready to write. (If this is you, feel free to skip to the next essay.) However, there are an equal number of writers who are unsure of what to write about. The thing to remember is that ideas can come from anywhere and are literally *everywhere*. Many professional writers keep a small notebook with them at all times, in order to jot down observations of the people and situations they see while running errands, exercising outside, or socializing. Zeroing in on someone who seems intriguing is a great way to start your brain working on a story, by imagining what that person's life is like, what the major conflict might be for them, and how that conflict could play out. As novelist and screenwriter William Goldman wrote in one of his books: "Life is material."

One of the best and most fun ways to gather new ideas is via writing exercises. An online search for writing exercises will lead you to dozens if not hundreds of great suggestions. Below are three exercises I've used myself or recommended to students. These involve making lists, which I'll talk about more in "The Power of Lists" in the Troubleshooting section. Lists are a great way to keep your analytical left brain busy, which will allow your creative right brain come out:

1. **Make a list of 50 possible movie titles.** If you have a tendency to lean toward one genre (for instance, all your titles have the words "Blood" or "Death" in them), try shaking up your brain by listing ten romantic comedy titles, ten sci-fi action titles, ten coming-of-age drama titles, etc.

2. **Make a list of 20 (or more) relationships**. Try to be specific: Instead of father/daughter, make it a widowed single father with twin four-year-old

daughters. Time yourself and try to write them as quickly as possible. You should be able to list 20 relationships in five minutes. Don't stop writing. Let the pairs be ridiculous if they need to be. The characters don't have to be contemporary or even human. Once you're done, go back and try to flesh the relationships out a little more: add ages, professions, personality traits, etc. Pick two or three you're the most drawn to or that seem to have the most dramatic potential and figure out the conflict in the relationship. Is one of these conflicts enough to fuel the start of a script?

3. <u>Make brainstorming flashcards.</u> On individual index cards, write down ten different professions, ten settings, ten obstacles, and ten goals. Shuffle each of the four decks, and pick one card from each. Write the opening scene of a screenplay based on these four elements. Repeat at least three times. Add to the decks over time, and come up with ideas for new decks: villains, time periods, love interests, etc.

Some writers fear that using an exercise to jumpstart a plot or developing a random stranger into a character will result in an impersonal story. However, the characters and storyline you develop will be fueled by your unique sensibility and experience. The same writing exercise can spark everything from a romantic comedy plot to a historical thriller, based on who is developing it. The old saying, "ideas are a dime a dozen," is true. The way you spin the idea, and your distinctive voice, will make the story one of a kind.

BEYOND THE PREMISE:
HOW TO DEVELOP A COMPELLING STORY

Many screenplays begin promisingly: a clever idea with inventive characters placed in an original situation. Then, about halfway into the script, the pace begins to sag, the character development stalls, and the plot grows increasingly repetitive. The promise of the opening is not fulfilled.

How do you take your concept and expand it into a complex, multi-dimensional story that a reader will recommend, and that a producer or studio will want to buy? Try one of the following methods:

1. **Have the set-up lead to a relationship for the protagonist that complicates the protagonist's goals**. Most screen stories have some sort of central relationship, but in the ones that work best, this relationship evolves directly out of the premise. In other words, these two people never would or could have hooked up if not for what happens in this plot.

For example, in WORKING GIRL, Melanie Griffith's character begins as a lowly secretary. It's only after deciding to pose as her boss that she's put in a position to meet Harrison Ford's character. However, the two do not simply embark on a sweet, conflict-free affair. Becoming involved with Ford makes Griffith's life more difficult for two major reasons: 1) it's Ford's company whom Griffith is playing her "con" out on. If she's exposed, it will hurt not only her but him as well, and she knows this. 2) Ford turns out to be dating Griffith's boss, the very woman Griffith is posing as, making it doubly difficult for Griffith to maintain the charade.

2. **Create a reversal in the protagonist's situation**. One of the best ways to keep an audience on its toes and involved in your story is to suddenly

spin the plot in a new direction. In this scenario, the set-up leads the audience to predict a certain pattern of events, only to thwart their expectations as the plot suddenly shifts gears. This shift usually takes place at page 45 or 60. In LAURA, what begins as a routine murder investigation takes on a new angle when the detective played by Dana Andrews learns that the woman he thought was killed is still alive; it was a different girl who had been slain. Now the detective must not only solve the original crime, he also has to protect Laura from her would-be murderer.

3. **Resolve the protagonist's problem halfway through, and have this resolution lead to a new goal for the protagonist**. If you get the sense that you're dragging out the action too long; or if you feel your story is too thin; or if you have a genre story that isn't diverging enough from the traditional formula, try wrapping up the plot early, but in such a way that it leaves the protagonist at the opposite point from where you intend them to end up. In THE LADY EVE, Barbara Stanwyck's con artist character and Henry Fonda's millionaire are meant to end up together. In lesser hands, the entire story would have taken place on the cruise ship where card sharp Stanwyck tries to bilk Fonda, only to fall for him. That approach would have risked the plot growing increasingly dull and predictable, however, as we waited for Fonda to find out the truth, dump Stanwyck, and then forgive her and reconcile with her at the end. However, writer-director Preston Sturges keeps one step ahead of the audience by having Fonda's discovery and rejection of Stanwyck take place halfway into the movie. The second half of the film then begins with the heartbroken Stanwyck embarking on a new goal: to get revenge on Fonda by wooing him in disguise and then breaking his heart.

4. **Introduce a new element into the plot**. The easiest way to elevate your story to a higher level is to simply add an element to the plot. In order for this method not to seem contrived, the event should emerge organically

from the story and not out of left field. It should also create conflict for the protagonist. A clear example of this is in GONE WITH THE WIND, where Scarlet O'Hara's romantic aspirations are complicated by the obstacles brought on by the outbreak of the Civil War. The new element can also be character-related. In THE GRADUATE, Dustin Hoffman's affair with Anne Bancroft is made more difficult when Katherine Ross, playing Bancroft's daughter, arrives on the scene.

5. **Change the genre**. With this method, it's essential that the transition be made carefully and slowly, so that the change in tone is inevitable rather than jarring. In LAURA, in addition to the reversal discussed above, the movie evolves from a murder mystery into a romance (although the suspense continues throughout), as Dana Andrews falls in love with Laura, first through the stories he hears from the people who knew her, and then in person when she reappears. More common are films that begin as straight drama and switch into thriller or suspense mode halfway in. (More on playing with genres in the next essay.)

An imaginative premise will hook your readers, but in order to hold their interest, you need surprising plot and character developments. What all these strategies have in common is that they increase the conflict, by making the protagonist's life more difficult. Conflict leads to tension, and tension is what makes a story compelling. If you apply these techniques, the result will be an original, inventive, and unpredictable screenplay—one that is much more likely to succeed commercially and critically.

REINVENTING THE WHEEL:
HOW TO TRANSCEND A GENRE

Another way to come up with new stories, or to develop the germ of one you've landed on, is to play around with genre. Executives and story analysts read so many romantic comedies, crime dramas, and thrillers that they know the formulas for these genres by heart. While most successful Hollywood movies can be easily classified by genre, many of the films that excel both critically *and* commercially do more than just connect the dots. Making your genre screenplay stand out involves attention to craft issues discussed in other chapters in this book (such as avoiding clichés in the plot and characterization, as well as strengthening supporting characters, and not letting structure dictate the action). What follows here, however, are several things to consider *before* you begin developing your story.

1. **<u>Combine genres</u>.** A common use of this approach is to take a genre plot and reinvent it as a science fiction story. The most notable example of this is STAR WARS, which is a western set in space. The fun of such blended genres for the reader and audience is in seeing how the writer adapts the source genre's beats to fit a fantastical world. Other examples of combined genres include WHAT WE DO IN THE SHADOWS, which inventively twists its vampire plot to work as a wry mockumentary as well, and GET OUT, in which the supernatural thriller storyline and the sociopolitical satire on race relations are perfectly intertwined, with each genre fueling the plot of the other. Beware of randomly tossing genres together, however. The action must fit naturally in both worlds in order to avoid seeming gimmicky and/or contrived.

2. **<u>Add romance to a genre plot</u>**. This is a specific application of the genre combination, and it's most often seen with suspense plots. While

many crime dramas and thrillers have their leads involved in a love affair, the romantic relationships tend to be minor subplots. However, putting romance and suspense on equal footing can raise an ordinary crime story to a new level. One example is CHARADE, which pairs suspense with romantic comedy. Another is WITNESS, which combines a dramatic love story with a police thriller. In the latter type of blend, the characters and their relationship must be written with a lot of complexity and originality in order to prevent the romantic plot from coming across as a melodramatic add-on. Another classic example is LAURA, which mixes murder mystery with romance. THE SHAPE OF WATER is both romance and science fiction drama. GOSFORD PARK blends mystery and romance—and then mixes in yet another genre: drawing-room comedy.

3. <u>Set the story in an unexpected time period or location</u>. Similar to the idea of combining genres, this tactic can intrigue the reader (and later the film audience) by piquing curiosity about how a familiar story will play out in the new setting. BLADE RUNNER is a cop thriller set in the future, for example. SHAKESPEARE IN LOVE is a romantic comedy set in Elizabethan England.

4. <u>Spin a genre plot around an unusual element</u>. One of the best examples of this is MEMENTO, which takes the concept of a man with short-term memory loss (ordinarily the stuff of an issue-based TV melodrama) and uses it as the basis for a thriller.

5. <u>Complicate the plot</u>. TOOTSIE transcends the "man in drag" formula by combining the expected gags with a series of well-developed, character-driven subplots, which are cleverly woven into the main storyline. THE USUAL SUSPECTS ratchets up the suspense by having flashbacks within flashbacks that shift suspicion from one character to the next, confusing the audience while still managing to hold their attention up to the final twist. Many romantic comedies today have rejected the old model of women looking specifically for love. One of the first to break this norm exceptionally well was WORKING GIRL, in which Melanie Griffith's character is focused solely on boosting her career and isn't interested in love. She finds romance anyway, but it's a by-product of her main goal.

6. Have your main character act "out of character." In LETHAL WEAPON, Mel Gibson is not the usual strong, stoic, and moralistic cop. He's suicidal, foolish, and careless. This gives the script and film an added level of tension. Although the story is a typical buddy-cop plot, the behavior of Gibson's character is unpredictable.

In writing any genre story, you'll still likely be following the basic formula for that type of story—or else it will no longer be a genre piece. What you want to avoid is having words like "predictable," "formulaic," "contrived," "by-the-book," "derivative," and/or "generic" show up in the coverage of your script (or later in a review of your movie). The way to do this is to begin with a solid foundation, even if it's a stock one, and then build an original story onto that foundation. Allow the plot to unfold organically, rather than obsessively following the typical beats of your base formula, and make sure you populate the action with rich and complex characterizations. You also want to make sure the story reflects your unique voice, style, and point of view. Just as an inventive architectural approach to a traditional edifice catches your eye, an inventive approach to a traditional screen story will catch the attention of readers, agents, and movie executives.

JUST WRITE A DRAFT

When I was in film school, there was one lesson I wish the instructors had taught us, and that's the importance of getting an entire rough draft out quickly, no matter how messy it ends up being, or how many gaps are in it. Writing the first draft is not the time to labor over problems, tweak characterizations, or polish prose. It may seem counterintuitive, but in my experience, you'll end up with a finished screenplay a lot more quickly if you write the first draft fast and then revise it several times than if you try to perfect the first draft as you're writing it.

There are many reasons for this, and they mainly revolve around the need to let your subconscious do a lot of the work at this stage. If you start revising and "fixing" too early, you'll prevent the freshest and most imaginative stuff from coming out. You'll also stop yourself from finding out what the story is *really* about. With few exceptions, I've found that in a first draft, whether it's mine or another writer's, the heart of the plot isn't revealed until the end—at which point many of the earlier sections of the script need to be revised so that this ending works.

There's an old story about Michelangelo explaining that he sculpted a horse by starting with a block of clay (or marble or stone, depending on the version of the story) and then cutting away everything that wasn't a horse. This is a great metaphor for artistic creation, and over time in my writing career I've added to it. Because, before you even have that block of clay, you have to *build* that block of clay—and before you can build the block of clay, you need to *dig up* the materials for it.

The digging up is the sifting through the dirt and twigs of your idea scraps to gather the characters and basic plot beats that you've decided will be part of the script you want to write. Then, once you have the dirt, you have to mix that with water to *make* the clay and shape it into that block. This is what you're doing with the first draft. In later drafts, as you revise, you'll begin shaping the clay, slowly carving away the parts that don't fit and polishing those that do, until you arrive at the final version.

What about an outline, you ask? To stick with the metaphor, an outline is a mix of gathering the materials and sifting, and also of making the clay, depending on how detailed of an outliner you are. Most screenwriters do write outlines. In fact, outlines are required if you're hired for a writing assignment. In an outline, you break the action down roughly into acts and sequences. An outline might also include some of the scenes within the sequences, and many writers use index cards for this. (More on sequences in the "Sequences: The Building Blocks of Your Script" in the Structure section.) There are plenty of screenwriting books that focus almost entirely on how to develop the basic structure for your script, and I'd advise any beginning writer to consult one or more of these. I've listed my favorites in the Appendix.

Outlines almost always change, however, so you don't want to spend *too* much time on them. To switch metaphors for a moment, think of the outline as a road map. It gives you the basic direction, as well as a destination, with a list of some of the stops along the way—but as with any trip, there will be unexpected detours and road blocks. Once you start writing the draft, new characters will appear, while some of those from your outline will be cut. Characters may make unexpected decisions; new actions will occur. You may realize your destination is something other than what you originally thought. The map is not the journey. It's a guide for the journey. The journey is the scenery, the experiences, the surprises, the people you meet, the things you discover, what you learn and how you've changed by the end of it, often in ways you could never have expected. If you spend all your time on the map, you'll never actually get anywhere.

Some writers are stronger on character and some are better at plotting, and this will come through in your first draft. There's nothing wrong with either approach, as long as you take the time to focus on the other element when you revise. If you tend to start with a character, I'd advise quickly reading through the essays in the Plot and Structure sections before starting your script, just so you're aware of the pitfalls you might in encounter. Conversely, if you're more of a plotter, you might want to look at the essays in the Character section. Being aware of the problems discussed in those essays may help your subconscious address some of them as you write. If you identify a problem, don't let it slow you down, however. Take notes on the issues that come up, so you can tackle them later when you revise, and *keep writing*.

The key thing to remember when writing the first draft is that it's the *first* draft, not the finished product. There's a reason why it's called a "rough" draft. The dictionary definition of "rough" is: "full of irregularities...not smooth...coarse, shaggy, uneven in texture...lacking polish or finesse...*not perfected or completed*." (Italics mine.) If you find yourself slowing down and obsessing over scenes or beats, just push on. Skip over gaps and fill them in later. I have two mantras I use when I hit these types of obstacles: "small problem" and "next draft." Don't censor yourself and don't let your inner critic start to judge you at this stage. It's okay in the first draft to let a scene go on too long, to let the dialogue be clunky. Remember, you're sometimes still making clay, or still digging up the dirt for the clay. These characters, this story, and this world didn't even *exist* only a short time ago. You therefore shouldn't expect that you'll know *everything* about these elements yet. The first draft is also often called the "discovery" draft, because you'll only discover who these characters really are, what they really want, and why they really want it once they come alive on the page.

Keep reminding yourself that you created these characters and this world *out of thin air*. That's pretty amazing! Pat yourself on the back. Then go back to work, and finish the draft.

TWO PEAS IN A POD: AVOIDING CLICHÉS

Certain situations, characters, and jokes are used over and over again in films. They're stock; formulaic; clichéd. When you use a cliché, you employ characters and conceits that thousands of other writers have used before you. By the time these hackneyed elements reach your script, they're tired, boring, and ultimately damaging to your story. If you count up the number of times you've seen a familiar plot point or action set piece in a movie, you can be sure the average story analyst or movie executive has encountered this cliché a dozen times more in the scripts they've read.

It's easy to resort to a cliché, because it's usually the first thing that comes to mind. It's familiar; it's the obvious choice. This is due to the fact that clichés often have a basis in reality. For example, there really are older people who are cranky. There *are* kids who are precocious. However, by caving in to these generalizations you risk offending or annoying your audience, and even worse, you short-change your story, by robbing it of the original point-of-view that only you can bring to it.

Sometimes it's necessary to allow clichés in some places when you're powering through your rough draft, so that you don't slow yourself down by questioning everything you're writing. However, this essay is useful to read now, so you can keep these issues in mind as you write. Then, after you have that first draft, come back to this essay.

Characters: Look closely at your characters and see if their actions are the result of the unique personality you've created for them, or if their behavior is simply what you'd expect because you've seen it before. Every character in your script should receive this attention. The best way to break through clichés in characterization is to constantly study the people you meet and know. Everyone has at least one thing about them that doesn't fit the puzzle. A scholarly, introspective person will suddenly display a talent for balloon animals. A giggling party girl will be an expert on horticulture. These unexpected traits give a character depth and credibility. In reality, no two people are exactly alike, and therefore no two characters should be alike either.

Setting: There will always be movies set in Los Angeles and New York City, especially if they're about Hollywood or Wall Street. However, be aware that movies about Hollywood and Wall Street are innately clichéd because of their settings. If you've chosen this subject matter, make sure you have a fresh angle for your story. If your script is simply an urban tale, try setting it in a city we don't see much on film: Pittsburgh or Houston, for example. Then do your research and add details to the story that are unique to that location. This will automatically add texture to your story, because the setting becomes a distinctive character in the piece.

Plot twists: The police captain is corrupt; the best friend is a traitor; it was all a dream. A professional reader or experienced moviegoer can see these dramatic bombshells coming before you've even lit the fuse. One way to keep the suspense alive is by sleight of hand. Just like a magician, keep the reader's attention diverted by other plot or character developments, so that the big revelation really does surprise. Another tactic is to milk every moment for suspense. If there are three main suspects in a serial killer script, make sure that all of them are, at one moment or another, a *genuinely* credible suspect.

Romantic entanglements: It's a joke among readers that the hero and heroine in a script always seem to have sex on page 70. While this may actually make sense structurally, don't throw the leads into bed together just because that's what's "supposed to happen" in the middle of the second act. Develop their relationship believably, so that their tryst doesn't feel contrived. Or consider increasing the dramatic and emotional tension by keeping them *out* of the sack.

You can certainly come up with dozens of other clichés on your own. Make lists of them: the crash through the store window; the chase to the top of the water tower; the fight on the catwalk. And then avoid using them, or find a way to spin them on their heads, so they still shock, surprise, and/or amuse. Stay ahead of your audience and they'll love you for it.

THEME

I struggled with whether to include this essay early in the book, because I don't believe you should be worrying or even thinking about theme when you're developing your story. A lot of writers ask about theme early on, however, and so I've placed the essay here—but this is definitely another essay to come back to later, after you've written at least one draft.

There are many definitions and interpretations of the hazy concept of theme. Is it a lesson to be taught? An attitude? How does it relate to the story's premise? Can you write a story that doesn't have a theme?

I consider theme as the author's underlying point of view about the story —and about life. The theme of an action movie is not "good versus evil." That merely describes the plot. The theme is a specific *perspective* on the sequence of events of the movie, such as "good *triumphs* over evil." Or, in the case of a dark thriller like CHINATOWN, the theme is the opposite: "evil triumphs over good." In the best movies, you can boil such broad concepts down even further. In CHINATOWN, the theme could also be interpreted as "wealth equals power."

Movies are stories and the important thing to remember is that no matter what the theme is, it must be expressed *in action*. Avoid having your characters state the theme explicitly. You *can* slip it in subtly, however. Viki King, in her book, "How to Write a Movie in 21 Days," suggests that the theme is usually stated in some form around page 3 of a screenplay. As an example, she points to Jake Gittes' line in CHINATOWN: "You have to be rich to get away with murder." It's important to note that the plot doesn't stop so Jake can make this pronouncement. It's just a throwaway line within the context of the action of the scene. Only when you go back and analyze the screenplay does the foreshadowing of the theme in this line become clear.

The thematic question is usually acted out via the dramatic question. In CHINATOWN, Jake, Jack Nicholson's detective character, is hired to solve a case that leads him to uncover more and more layers of corruption and immorality. "Will Jake solve the case he's been hired for?" becomes "Can good possibly triumph over pure evil?" The theme is also reflected in other aspects of a film, from the characterization to the plot to the setting to the imagery. For example, CHINATOWN's theme is echoed in its Los Angeles setting, a city that steals water from its poorer neighbors.

It's usually not until the end of your first draft that the theme becomes clear. You can then use this knowledge to unify your action. Find places where the theme can be reflected in a subplot, in a comic gag, or in the use of weather and location. However, be wary of laying on thematic elements too heavily or you may push your story into corny melodrama, or make it come across as pretentious and contrived.

You don't have to think too hard about theme when you're starting the script, however—and in fact, as I stated above, you *shouldn't*. The theme will emerge in how your characters behave and react, whether you plan it or not. If you begin with the theme and then construct a plot to fit it, you'll end up with a sermon not a story. Also, never try to impose a theme on your story. If the action is saying "Love stinks" and you try to force a happy ending, this resolution isn't going to ring true. Respect the integrity of your story as it exists and work to strengthen and clarify its theme, not nullify it.

Every writer has their own belief system, and this attitude toward the world will naturally emerge in any story they tell. Always begin with a character in a dramatic situation. How the character behaves in response to that situation, and the ramifications of their actions, will illustrate your distinctive perspective—and *that* will determine your theme.

III. <u>CHARACTERIZATION</u>

Ask most writers, producers, and film executives, and they'll say characterization is the most important element in any screenplay. The most "high concept" idea will flop if the characters are dull and derivative, while a straightforward genre plot will excel if the characters are complex, compelling, and unlike any we've seen before. This is largely because exceptional characterizations can lure top actors to the project. Rich characters will also result in an emotionally gripping story that will draw audiences to the resulting film—and, in the case of great characters, will cause viewers to want to watch the movie again and again. Strong characterization, even with a weak script, can lead to a script sale, or, at the very least serve as a successful writing sample. The essays in this section will help you address characterization problems you may encounter as you write your script, as well as help you deepen and sharpen those characters once you have a draft.

FLAWED PROTAGONISTS
CHARACTER ARC
ACT NOT REACT
HOW TO LURE A CHARACTER OUT OF HIDING
SUPPORTING CHARACTERS: THE CORNERSTONE OF YOUR
SCRIPT
DIALOGUE

FLAWED PROTAGONISTS

Writers are often reluctant to give their protagonists any flaws, especially if these characters are intended to be heroes. However, a reader or viewer will have difficulty warming up to characters who lack vulnerability, who never make mistakes or doubt themselves, and/or never demonstrate any negative traits.

A character can be a good person without being perfect. True heroes, after all, are mortals who transcend their own human frailties and fears. In fact, the more human your characters, the more an audience will identify with and root for them. Weaknesses make a character sympathetic, interesting, complex, and real. Flaws also give characters dimension and therefore make them more intriguing.

A flawed protagonist sets the stage for one of the key elements of a success-ful screenplay: the character arc. (More on character arc in the next essay.) It's impossible for a character who's already perfect to change or grow dur-ing the course of the story; there will therefore be little reason to root for them emotionally. Triumph over adversity is much more dramatically satis-fying if the hero has to overcome personal demons as well as external obsta-cles in order to achieve it. In CASABLANCA, for instance, Humphrey Bogart's character conquers his own cynicism and bitterness, making him willing to risk his life to save his former lover and her husband. In THE BRIDGE ON THE RIVER KWAI, William Holden plays a conniving, self-serving sailor who is forced against his will to participate in a deadly mission, but who ultimately gives his life for a greater cause. The title char-acter in SCHINDLER'S LIST begins as an apolitical German business-man, and by the end he's forfeited his selfish desire for financial gain in order to save the lives of his Jewish workers. It's no coincidence that all three of these movies won the Academy Award for Best Picture—and for Best Screenplay.

Moral flaws that are at odds with the characters' roles as "heroes" in the story can be the most challenging to write, but they often make for the most interesting and memorable characters. In L.A. CONFIDENTIAL, Russell Crowe's character is a staunch defender of battered women yet he also suffers from a barely contained violent streak—a trait that inevitably leads him to beat up Kim Basinger's character. He's as horrified by his actions as the audience is, and his conflicted, complex personality pulls us more deeply into the drama. One of the most intriguing elements of the original CAPE FEAR is the fact that Gregory Peck's law-abiding attorney begins to behave unethically when he tries to have Robert Mitchum's character run out of town—even hiring a group of men to beat up Mitchum at one point. Although Mitchum's character *is* truly a bad guy who needs to be stopped, this initial moral ambiguity makes the film more than just a standard revenge story. Movies like these are also compelling because the characters' flaws make their actions less predictable; we're not always sure they'll do the right thing.

A protagonist's weakness can add further tension to the plot by acting as an obstacle to their own goal. In CLUELESS, Alicia Silverstone's character wants to solve everyone's problems (usually romantic), but her myopia concerning what's really best for those around her often causes her to lead her victims further away from their hearts' desires. This need for total control backfires on her personally, when she pairs herself with the wrong guy. (In the novel *Emma* by Jane Austen, which inspired CLUELESS, the main character has the same flaw.) A darker version of this can be seen in A SIMPLE PLAN, in which Bill Paxton's greed causes him to make one bad decision after another, leading him deeper and deeper into tragedy.

Even bigger-than-life characters need flaws in order to prevent them from ending up one-dimensional cartoons. Superman would not be as interesting if not for: a) Kryptonite, and b) his alter ego's crippling shyness and insecurity. Movies that seem to be pure action can be made a little bit more real and immediate by giving the main character a weakness of some kind. A famous example of this is Harrison Ford's fear of snakes in RAIDERS OF THE LOST ARK.

A character's flaws, whether they be moral weaknesses, superstitions, fears, neuroses, insecurities, or prejudices, are as important as their strengths or external qualities such as age and gender—perhaps more so. Vulnerabilities are what make us human and what make us unique. Allowing your characters to have human shortcomings will help you bring a fictional creation to living, breathing life.

CHARACTER ARC

Every story, in every medium, contains a change of some kind. The journey from beginning to middle to end is the very definition of this shift. A situation and a character begin as one thing and end as another, and the middle is the path that links these two points. In the best stories, this path is not a straight line. It's a development that builds as it goes: an arc.

The character arc can be one of the most challenging elements of a screenplay, and yet it's one of the most essential. Many promising screenplays begin with a good idea and interesting characters, but in the course of the story, while things may "happen," nothing essential changes for the protagonist. If you break down most good film plots, you'll find a shift in values of some kind for the protagonist. A bad man becomes good; a good man turns bad. A coward transforms into a hero; a shy wallflower becomes a confident success story. The arc is never arbitrary. It's intrinsic to the story and it informs the action. It supports the theme and is inherent in the premise.

Character dramas are the easiest films to analyze for character arcs, with the coming-of-age film being the most obvious. The young protagonist encounters various dramatic situations that lead them to become more mature as a result. In EIGHTH GRADE, for example, the teenage protagonist begins as desperately needing acceptance and attention; she gradually learns, mainly via encounters with a number of self-centered and often cruel peers, that what really matters is that she accepts and respects *herself*. She's also initially rebellious towards her loving father but eventually grows up enough to realize he's the one person who is genuinely on her side.

Some genres are practically defined by their familiar arcs. In many traditional romantic comedies, the playboy learns to commit, the uptight career woman loosens up and finds love, or the shy protagonist gains confidence and pursues the object of their affection. In westerns, the misanthropic loner ends up saving a town from the bad guys, or a weakling is forced to take a stand against the villain. Ideally, as I discussed earlier in "Two Peas in a Pod," you'll want to find a way to subvert this predictability in order for your screenplay to stand out from others in the same genre. The best way to do this is to dig more deeply into your characters in order to find the inner struggle that is unique to them and use *that* to inform the character's arc.

Building the character arc in your story is a matter of careful development. Scripts where a character suddenly changes or "sees the light" in the last scene ring false and are not likely to win over readers or audiences. A character transformation must be gradual, deliberate, and believable. Ideally, each sequence should move the character forward in some way. One way to think of this is as "lessons learned." For instance, in TOOTSIE, Dustin Hoffman's character begins as a self-centered womanizer and temperamental actor. In the first act, he disguises himself as a woman in order to get a role on a soap opera, and he meets and falls for Jessica Lange's character, his co-star. Hoffman gains empathy for women when the soap's director treats him patronizingly and when finds himself stalked by the soap's lecherous leading man. He also discovers that as a woman, he handles conflict better, and he's able to put his ego aside and concentrate on his craft. He gets to know Jessica Lange as a friend, not just as a potential sexual conquest, and he matures emotionally as a result. Each sequence of the movie revolves around one or more events that teach Hoffman about women, about sexism, and about himself, so that by the end of the movie, he's a changed man.

In action fare, the arc is usually prompted by a series of tests. In STAR WARS, Luke Skywalker begins as a naïve, sheltered, and immature kid. The sudden and brutal deaths of his guardians thrust him out onto his own. As the plot unfolds, Luke faces one challenge after another, and each challenge contains increasing danger and higher stakes. Each test forces Luke to grow up a little, to take more responsibility for himself and his goals, and to become more self-reliant.

There are movies where the central character does not have a significant character arc. In these films, their role serves mainly to change those around them: they cause character arcs rather than undergoing one themselves. Examples include superhero movies and sports films in which a wise coach comes in to help a struggling team. However, superhero franchises almost always begin with an origin story in which we *do* see the character change and come to accept their new role. In the best sports underdog movies, such as BAD NEWS BEARS, the coach also changes over the course of the story.

Discussions of character arc often include the concepts of want vs. need. What the protagonist wants is the goal that drives their actions, and is what they believe will lead them to their happily-ever-after. (This applies even if the character's goal is something dark like revenge.) What they need relates to their inner issue, and what they need to learn—which their journey over the course of the story will teach them. For instance, in TOOTSIE, Dustin Hoffman wants success as an actor at all costs. This is what he thinks will make him happy. What he *needs* is to learn how to connect emotionally with others. By the end of the story, he gives up his initial want, now that he understands that this need is what will truly make him happy. Your protagonist doesn't have to give up their initial want, however. In 127 HOURS, James Franco's loner character learns over the course of the story he needs other people, yet he maintains his life-and-death goal of getting free of the crevasse he's fallen into.

When you're working on your screenplay and are faced with a sequence or passage that feels emotionally empty or uninvolving, it's often because the action has become disconnected from the character. Study and analyze these troublesome passages. Is there a way in which the events of the sequence could challenge the character's perception of himself? Would it work better to have them make a difficult, even uncharacteristic decision at the end of the sequence? Could they learn something that alters their behavior? Does their view of another character change?

Refocus the action so it's prompted by the characters' choices and growth. This will make your characters more than just props in the plot, and the result will be a more emotionally involving story. This in turn will make your screenplay more appealing to actors, as well as one that's more likely to engage readers—and later your audience.

ACT NOT REACT

One of the most common complaints story analysts make about the scripts they pass on is that the protagonist isn't active enough. Most writers know that their protagonists shouldn't be passive. A character who fails to take action, who is acted upon by others, or who lacks a dramatic goal of any kind, is difficult to either become engaged by or root for. However, it gets tricky when it seems as if your lead is acting when in truth they are simply *reacting* to events or to the actions of other characters. A protagonist who is merely reactive is not much better than a passive character.

An active character drives the story. It's their choices and actions that propel the plot forward. Achieving this as a writer is easiest in genre plots like action-adventures or thrillers. Characters such as Indiana Jones and Iron Man are active by definition. It's more challenging to keep your lead active in less overtly breathtaking genres, like dramas and relationship stories. However, it's possibly even more important in these types of scripts to make sure your protagonist is as active as possible, because it is they and not the events that will be providing the drama for the story.

There are different levels of activism in film heroes. Some protagonists enter the story with a clear goal. A teenage boy may want to leave home or win over a girl or boy at his school. The film then follows the protagonist on this quest, as he faces various hurdles and either succeeds or fails. Often a new goal may replace or be added to the original goal midway into the story, adding depth to the plot and increasing the tension. In some films, the main character may not commit to their principal goal for the story until near the end of the first act. For instance, a criminal kills a cop's family in the first sequence, and the cop later sets out to get revenge. However, even if the central tension of the story kicks in later, your character should still be active in the early scenes. Have them be after *something*: the cop is trying to solve a different crime, for example; the teenage boy is trying to keep his failing grades a secret from his parents. Ideally, this initial goal will tie into or complicate the protagonist's main goal at some point.

What you want to be especially wary of is the character whose actions are motivated by the actions of others. A character may be on the run from a villain but only act when forced to by the villain; the protagonist never comes up with a set plan to escape the villain and instead merely reacts to events as they occur. As a result, the villain ends up the more active character and therefore the more compelling one. Stories like this often seem to be perpetually on the verge of starting but never actually do. Sometimes, the hero may finally come up with a plan in the third act, but this is too late. The plan needs to come in the first act—even if it changes later—because the ramifications of that initial plan are what should be driving the second act. If the plan doesn't show up until the third act, the first two acts end up coming across as merely an overwritten set-up.

The main tension of a script is always tied into the main character's goal. Constantly ask yourself: what does your protagonist want and why? How are they planning to achieve it? What is standing in their way? What *specifically* is the audience rooting for? Your character has to want something, even if it's something more emotionally-driven such as a healed relationship or peace of mind, and they need to have a plan to achieve it. Without a goal, the character is merely a puppet and unlikely to engage a reader or audience.

HOW TO LURE A CHARACTER OUT OF HIDING

As you develop your screenplay, you'll inevitably find that there are one or two characters who remain stubbornly elusive no matter how many character biographies you write or how hard you try to "put yourself in the character's place." The character biography *can* be a useful tool, but the information you get this way consists mainly of dry facts. Think of how you get to know someone new. You could ask them all the questions you ask in a character biography: "Where did you go to school?" "What was your relationship with your parents like?" This will give you information, but it's only superficial information, and there's no way of knowing for sure if the answers you're getting are true. So how do you get to know the *real* person?

Here are a few suggestions:

1. Spy on them when they're alone. Write a scene in which only the character you're having trouble with is present. How does the character behave when no one is watching? Does the character suddenly act differently? Are there vulnerabilities the character keeps hidden from the world? Are they uncomfortable with solitude, or does it provide them with the only opportunity they have in their life to "be themselves"?

2. Put them in direct conflict. When people are pushed against a wall, they'll often behave instinctively, betraying traits that are kept under wraps when everything is going well. Write a scene in which your character is thwarted or threatened by another character or obstacle. Do they instantly fight back, or do they keep their emotions in check until they finally explode? What verbal slips do they make in the heat of the moment that betray how they really feel about the situation?

3. <u>Seduce them</u>. Write a scene in which your character is seduced by something or someone they've tried to resist. This can be a sexual seduction or it can be another type of thrill: gambling, food, crime, etc. Figuring out what secretly turns your character on can illuminate a hidden aspect that might otherwise never be seen.

4. <u>Cause them pain</u>. This can be physical or emotional pain. Exposing characters' vulnerabilities pushes them to act instinctively, and also shatters the façade they show to the world. This is why you often see love scenes in action movies where the romantic leads connect when one lead takes care of the other after the first has been injured. The injured party lowers their guard and is therefore able to open up emotionally.

5. <u>Put the character in the worst situation possible</u>. Write a scene in which the character believes all is lost. This is when their deepest fears and strengths often emerge. One way to test the arc of a character is to write a scene that's related to what's happening at the start of your script, and then repeat the exercise for a time later in the story, to see if the character's actions have changed due to what they've experienced between the two points.

6. <u>Observe what others think about the character</u>. Write a scene in which the character you're working on isn't present. Observe how a friend, colleague, or family member feels about this character; what does the other person know about the character that the character doesn't show to the world? Ideally, you could write several of these scenes, starting with the people who are closest to the character, and then expanding to gauge the opinions of those who only know the character professionally, or in some other superficial way. Even strangers often have insight into people they don't know well, because they're able to see them objectively. (It's not necessary that these outside characters actually be part of the cast of your script.)

7. If all else fails, get them drunk. It's a truism that booze lowers inhibitions, but this truism can come in handy if your character simply refuses to let you into their head no matter what you throw at them. Write a scene in which your character gets drunk, and then put them together with any character in your script with whom they have a key relationship. This may uncover an emotion the character has been covering up. The character may tell the other off, or may declare their love, or they may apologize for a past action they'd always claimed was justified. You can also try pairing your inebriated character with someone not important to them, but who provides a willing, sympathetic ear, enabling the character to finally pour out feelings and thoughts that have been bottled up for years.

While these exercises are intended to be separate from the action of your screenplay, you may find that with a few tweaks some of these scenes actually have a place in the story. The important thing is that you come away feeling that you've gotten to know this elusive person better. This deeper understanding will show in the writing, when a formerly flat character comes to three-dimensional life.

SUPPORTING CHARACTERS:
THE CORNERSTONE OF YOUR SCRIPT

Much attention is paid by writers, directors, executives, and story analysts to developing a screenplay's lead characters into compelling, three-dimensional personalities. However, as much work should go into developing the supporting characters. When written well, these characters help define the main characters and add texture and dimension to the story.

All supporting characters are not created equal, however. There are different types, and each requires a different level of development. (The terms for some of these characters are occasionally used interchangeably—by myself included!—but I've broken them down into specific labels here for the purposes of analyzing each in more depth.)

One-String Characters: They're called one-string because they only sound one note in the story: the cranky landlady, the annoying co-worker, the precocious neighbor boy. These characters may fill out scenes, provide exposition, or add a comic touch. These characters don't necessarily advance the plot, however, nor do their relationships with the other characters change. To make your one-string character as memorable as possible, think in terms of giving the actor something juicy to play. William Goldman was a genius at this. In most of his scripts, most notably THE PRINCESS BRIDE, every character, no matter how small, has a "moment"—even if they're only present in one scene.

Be wary of the easy, clichéd choices, however, and try to find the most original (yet believable) trait possible. Don't go overboard. You don't want the character to come across as unbelievable or mannered, and you don't want them to dominate the action. In addition, be careful not to give one-string characters more depth than they need. If you provide the neighbor boy with a whole backstory and subplot of his own, your main plot will grind to a halt and you'll bore your audience. Recognize the one-string characters for who they are, consider providing them with one memorable trait, and then move on.

Minor Characters: These characters can have brief backstories or subplots of their own, as long as the subplot/backstory relates to or affects the main character. Unlike one-string characters, who are sometimes in danger of being overdeveloped, minor characters are often underdeveloped in scripts, making their presence seem contrived rather than organic to the story.

One helpful way to gauge the success of your minor characters is to use the "Rule of Three." Every minor character should have at least three beats in the story, which show an evolution or change of some kind. These can be the beats of the relationship with the main character, or beats of action, or beats of humor. For instance, an overbearing parent may first be seen berating their meek child (the hero of the story), then challenging the child's newfound independence, and finally being told off by the child and forced to accept a new, more mature relationship with them.

The Secondary Characters: These characters have larger roles than minor characters: the love interest in a romantic comedy, for example, or the villain in an action film. These characters should have fully developed backstories and subplots. A romantic comedy with a weak, undefined love interest falls flat. We don't care whether the hero lands their love interest, for example, if we don't know the love interest well enough to know if they're worth the effort. Similarly, a weak villain makes the hero's triumph unsatisfying.

Within the above categories certain types of individual characters stand out:

The Confidante: This is often a best friend, but they can also be a stranger the hero has just met, such as a bartender. This character acts as a sounding board for the hero to give voice to their goal in life (and in the story).

The "Raisonneur": This is the wise sage—a parent, an older friend, a co-worker, or a magical figure in a fantasy story—who defines what is right and wrong. The hero usually begins on the wrong side of the moral compass, but, via their experience during the course of the story, they ultimately see the light. The raisonneur may guide or just comment on this transformation.

The Naysayer: Although an antagonist, this is not the primary villain. The naysayer constantly gives the hero a hard time or puts them down. It could be a neighbor, a relative, or a co-worker, for instance. This character is one of the more minor figures, usually with no independent subplot, but they can play an important role, especially in a comedy, as someone who gets their comeuppance in the end and thereby underscores the hero's triumph. The naysayer may also come around to the hero's side in the end.

Although there are movies that focus solely on one character, in most films, a main character without sufficient support will come across as unreal and uninteresting. We're all defined by our friends and enemies, and by how we interact with those around us. Developing *all* of the characters in your script to their potential will result in a rich, authentic, and emotionally involving story.

DIALOGUE

Dialogue is one of the most important elements of developing your characters into distinctive and memorable creations. Dialogue is also one of the first things a reader notices. No matter how intriguing your idea or how well-structured the plot, if the dialogue is flat or doesn't ring true, the script is going to fall short of success. All writers can benefit from keeping several important points in mind when they're putting words into their characters' mouths:

1. <u>Avoid chunks</u>. As mentioned in "White Space" in the Nuts and Bolts section, long chunks of dialogue are considered unprofessional and are almost always unnecessary. While stage plays rely on dialogue to tell their stories, film is a visual medium and the dialogue needs to serve the action. If your characters tend to say more than five or six lines of dialogue at a time, go back and look at each exchange. Often, it's the first and/or last sentences that contain the meat of what the character is trying to say. Cut the rest. Occasionally, there are times when a monologue is called for, but it will be much easier to read and digest if broken into smaller segments. You can do this by inserting the reaction of another character, or by describing an action, activity, or gesture performed by the speaker.

2. <u>Avoid talking heads</u>. Overwritten conversations are another problem in many scripts. If you have one whole page or more with nothing but dialogue, then you've lost the visual sense of your screenplay. What are the characters doing? What's going on in the space? Try to find ways to insert action into these types of conversations.

3. <u>Avoid repetition</u>. You can often solve the above problem by eliminating repetitive statements. There's no need for characters to re-emphasize points or repeat arguments that have just been made. Figure out exactly what it is the characters *need* to say in the scene, get right to it, and move on.

4. Beware of "real" dialogue. Good movie dialogue is not how people really speak; it's an artful interpretation of how people speak. In real life, people hem and haw, repeat themselves, pause, and are often inarticulate. If you have a character who is intentionally inarticulate, their speech still needs to be carefully crafted so that it advances the scene and doesn't bog it down.

5. Beware "clever" dialogue. Conversely, you don't want dialogue that is so witty and arch that it comes across as artificial and takes the reader out of the reality of the story. Smart dialogue is always welcome, but it needs to emerge credibly from the character.

6. Voice. Ideally, every character should have their own unique manner of speech. There's no need for the differences to be extreme, but you want to avoid having everyone sound alike. The character's voice should also be consistent throughout the screenplay, as well as consistent with the character's background and personality. A shy person may be reserved and say little. An outgoing person may be verbose. However, you can also use voice in a way that contrasts believably with the character's background. For instance, characters trying to sound smarter than they actually may use fancy words but may employ them incorrectly.

7. Slang. Certain regions of the country and the world come with their own slang, as do different cultures and specific social circles such as gangsters and urban teens. Using slang in your script will give it an authentic feel. However, make sure that you: 1) use the slang correctly, 2) make it accessible, and 3) avoid having it sound clichéd. One false step and the attempt will come off as contrived or stereotypical.

8. Shorthand. As with slang, characters from a specific cultural or social group will often share phrases and idioms, like the con men in THE STING. Friends, family members, or colleagues often have distinctive expressions that develop from shared experiences over the course of the script, which become a sort of informal code. The movie THE APARTMENT is filled with this type of dialogue. Unique idioms help flesh out the world your characters live in and bring the audience into that world. As with other dialogue techniques, never try to force it and remember that a little goes a long way.

9. Agenda. Every line of dialogue in your script should have a dramatic purpose. The most common and effective purpose is to bring about a specific outcome. In every scene, the principal characters enter the action with a goal or intention, and that should be reflected in their speech. The drama of the scene comes from the obstacles to this goal, and again this should be reflected in the dialogue. In DOUBLE INDEMNITY, for example, Barbara Stanwyck's and Fred MacMurray's characters use dialogue both to manipulate each other and to defend themselves from being manipulated.

10. Comedy. Naturally, one would expect the dialogue in comedy scripts to be funny, but it always helps to have some wit and levity in more serious fare too. In real life, homicide detectives joke around to help counter the gloom and violence of their jobs, and friends and families often lighten a shared tragic event with humor.

11. Contractions. Lack of contractions often shows up in scripts by beginning writers. Your dialogue needs to sound conversational, not formal.

Look for places where "I am" and "You are" should be "I'm" and "You're," etc. One way to make sure your dialogue flows is to read your script aloud to yourself (or have someone read it aloud to you). This is a good idea for all writers, as it helps you not only catch examples of stilted speech but also overwritten or clunky dialogue passages that need to be tightened and polished.

In addition to reading your dialogue aloud, read produced writers' scripts. While eavesdropping on real people can help you get a flavor for how people with different backgrounds and different personalities talk, reading scripts will help you see how dialogue is crafted so it doesn't just reflect life but actually serves, advances, and enhances your story and characterizations.

IV. <u>STRUCTURE</u>

We're all natural storytellers. Any tale you tell, from a comical run-in with the clerk at the grocery store to a saga involving your time at sailing camp when you were eight years old, will inherently be told in a certain manner. There will be the set-up of the characters and setting, the introduction of one or more dramatic events, and then the development of these events, all tied up in a resolution. In other words: a beginning, a middle, and an end. Even movies in which the plot is told backwards or skips around in time still has this structure. The action may be on a different timeline, but the movie will still begin when it fades in and end when it fades out.

Structure is what holds a plot together. As I touched when discussing outlines in "Just Write a Draft," it's helpful to have a basic outline of your script's plot before you begin to write. Once you've completed a draft, you can dive into the structure more deeply. If the story seems to stall in certain areas, a knowledge of structure will help you build these areas up.

As I've mentioned, reading scripts and watching movies, and analyzing their structures, is one of the best ways to get better at this craft element. In the Appendix, I break down the structures of three well-known films: IT HAPPENED ONE NIGHT, RUSHMORE, and DIE HARD. You can also find examples of script breakdowns online, most notably on savethe-cat.com, where followers have applied the "beat sheets" in Blake Snyder's "Save the Cat" books to many famous films as well as TV shows.

The first essay included here is more informational in its description of film sequences. The remaining essays deal with structure problems, which have repeatedly turned up in the screenplays I've read over the years, broken down into the acts in which those problems appear.

SEQUENCES: THE BUILDING BLOCKS OF A SCRIPT
THE FIRST ACT: GETTING YOUR STORY STARTED
THE SECOND ACT: THE MEAT OF YOUR STORY
THE THIRD ACT: GOING OUT WITH A BANG

SEQUENCES: THE BUILDING BLOCKS OF A SCRIPT

In terms of story structure, a sequence is a dramatic unit with a clear beginning, middle and end, made up of scenes that are tied together thematically and dramatically. Taken as a whole, the sequence can be viewed as a concrete step in a dramatic staircase you're building from the beginning to the end of your screenplay. Within the script, each sequence plays a different role in the advancement of the characters and the story.

A sequence is a microcosm of the screenplay itself. Like the overall plot, it should begin with a dramatic situation, followed by an incident or revelation that complicates the situation and establishes the source of tension for the sequence. The action that ensues leads to a turning point and then to a resolution that brings about the next sequence.

Screenplays usually have eight sequences. This number evolved from the early days of cinema. A "two-reeler" was a short film of twenty minutes or less, because film reels held ten minutes of film each. Among these shorts were serials, in which each new episode had to clearly advance the ongoing story by the end of the reel. Longer feature films were made up of eight reels, and screen storytellers tended to structure their plots so that each reel contained a coherent dramatic unit, like the serials. Films have gotten longer over time, but the general structure of cinematic storytelling has remained fairly consistent.

In some films, it's easy to identify sequences. For instance, in THE STING, the sequences of the second and third acts are introduced by title cards: "The Set-Up," "The Hook," etc. This is a good way to approach your own sequences. Come up with eight figurative title cards that sum up your major plot points, and then structure the action accordingly. You don't need to actually use these title cards in your script, but they're a handy way to help you structure your scenes.

Another way to recognize sequences is that they often take place within a set period of time. After a sequence is completed, the ensuing sequence is then introduced with a visual clue that indicates the passage of time. We may see the young heroine now grown up, or the colorful fall leaves of the previous sequence may be replaced by bare branches covered in snow.

Sometimes a particular event acts as a sequence, such as an arrival, a departure, a wedding, or a sports competition. Big events like the final game in a sports movie or a major chase scene in an action film are also known as "set pieces." The "event" doesn't have to be momentous, however. It can be as simple as a confrontation or personal revelation. A notable change in the characters or in their relationships from the beginning to the end of the group of scenes is another trait of a sequence.

Although this may seem like a mechanical and emotionless way to approach a story, understanding sequences and their purpose can help you structure your story to maximum dramatic effect. Most screenwriters, no matter how new they are to the craft, tend to have an innate understanding of sequences, from years of watching movies. However, bringing this subconscious knowledge to the surface can help sharpen this natural ability and thereby strengthen your plot. This is especially true in the second act, where even experienced writers get bogged down under the burden of multiple subplots, advancing action, and ongoing character development.

That said, it's most helpful if you analyze your sequences *after* you have a draft. Trying to determine exactly where to begin or end a sequence can cause you to unnaturally force your plot or characters into a set design and rob you of the opportunity of discovering a surprising dramatic beat or character development you couldn't have foreseen before you began writing.

THE FIRST ACT: GETTING YOUR STORY STARTED

Most writers are aware of the importance of the first five to ten pages of a screenplay, which provide a first impression to agents and development executives. However, even if you manage to hook your reader with an exciting opening, you need to make sure they keep reading. Tight, compelling first acts that are integral parts of the whole story take work. Below are some key elements of the first act, and suggestions on how to deal with the challenges that come with them.

Exposition: Finding a dramatic way to express background information concerning your setting, story, and characters can be difficult. While you don't want your reader to be confused, you also don't want to stop the plot dead merely to relay a few facts.

One method of getting exposition across is to use conflict. Having characters reveal information as part of an argument automatically makes it more interesting. Conversely, if one character is desperately trying to get information from another character who is reluctant to give it, you create tension and therefore drama.

Another way to get exposition across cleverly is by having a principal character be a stranger or newcomer to the location. That character then stands in for the audience, who is similarly in the dark. The character's need to find out more about the setting, situation, and/or other characters becomes a logical part of the plot.

Whenever you do reveal information, try to do it in action. When exposition is executed well enough, the reader or audience will be too caught up on what is happening from scene to scene to realize the writer is also filling them in on the background of the characters, their situation, their relationships, and their world.

However, don't feel you have to tell the reader *everything* in the first act. Withholding information until it's absolutely necessary can create suspense and drama. For instance, we may learn early on that a young girl's mother has died, but not how. Waiting to reveal the details until it's essential builds tension, because the audience is waiting and wanting to know more. The delay also prevents the plot from getting bogged down with unnecessary information. Focus only on what's happening in the moment, and tell us only the minimal amount we need to understand the action.

Character set-up: Make sure you clearly establish who your protagonist is, why they are special, and why we should be interested in their story, within the first few pages. Many writers fail to distinguish the lead from the other characters quickly enough, and this makes it difficult to be drawn into the plot.

Another common weakness in character set-up is the inclusion of too many scenes demonstrating the protagonist's problem. For instance, if the script is about an alcoholic, beginning writers often include more than one scene of the lead's addiction getting them into trouble, with their family, for instance, or at work, *before* the actual story starts. Once you've shown us the character's problem, it's best to start the story as quickly as possible. Even better, have the revelation of their problem actually *be* the beginning of the plot. In THE STING, we aren't shown several scenes of Hooker, Robert Redford's con artist character, robbing marks with his partner and then blowing the money. Instead, the first con we see Hooker carry out is against an employee of crime lord Lonnegan, played by Robert Shaw. This action sets up a series of paybacks that fuel the entire plot of the film.

The point of attack: This is a key moment in the first act, and its absence is a notable flaw in some scripts. This beat is also sometimes called the "catalyst." This is the moment that causes the set-up to shift from a situation to a story. In THE STING, the murder of Hooker's partner is what spurs Hooker into wanting revenge. Without this event, the story wouldn't have evolved beyond Hooker being on the run from Lonnegan. Make sure you can clearly identify the point of attack in your script. (More on this in "Situation vs. Story.")

The turning point: You should also be able to clearly identify the end of the first act. This is when we know what the conflict is and also know very specifically what we're supposed to be rooting for. Simply: this is where the story begins. At the end of the first act in ELF, Buddy leaves the North Pole for New York City in order to find and reconcile with his father. In SCHOOL OF ROCK, the first act wraps up with Jack Black's character deciding to form a rock group with his elementary school students in order to compete in a battle of the bands.

A solid first act should propel the writer, the characters, and later the reader and audience into the second act, which I discuss in the next essay.

THE SECOND ACT: THE MEAT OF YOUR STORY

The first act is often the easiest thing to write in a first draft, because enthusiasm and energy are high, and you're still setting up the characters and situation. The real struggle comes in the second act, in developing these elements and keeping the plot consistently moving forward while tracking the protagonist's inner journey. Below are problems that frequently occur in second acts. All writers are faced with most of these in early drafts. The important thing is to recognize them and work hard to address them in your revisions.

Repetition: Scripts tend to sag in the second act because plot beats and character beats repeat themselves. The central tension has been set up but the action seems to run in place, as the hero and villain face off over and over, or the two romantic leads spar and make up over and over, or the protagonist makes several attempts to achieve their goal and hits one obstacle after another, with no change in their characterization or circumstances.

Make sure every scene and every sequence moves your story forward in some way. If the hero loses a battle with a villain, this must result in a change of some kind. For instance, the hero's ally may get killed, leaving the hero alone in their quest. Or the hero may gain an ally when one of the villain's lackeys joins them after the hero saves the lackey's life. In both cases, the protagonist's situation has changed significantly, forcing them to act in a new way and/or come up with a new strategy. This type of development keeps the story moving and the audience hooked.

Another form of repetition is when beats from the first act are rehashed in the second act. If the protagonist is shown in the first act to have a difficult relationship with their ex-spouse, for instance then any scene between the lead and their ex-spouse in the second act must reveal how the relationship and/or the protagonist and/or the protagonist's situation is changing as a result of each interaction, rather than merely demonstrate, yet again, that a conflict exists.

Magical appearing/disappearing characters: Often in a rough draft of a script, certain supporting characters introduced in the first act may fade from view in the second act, while new ones pop up. In rewriting it's important to identify these characters and either make them more substantial or drop them.

It's fine for "one-string characters" (defined in "Supporting Characters: The Cornerstone of Your Script") who are only necessary for a specific plot beat—such as a clerk in a store—appear only once or twice in the script. However, if a character is introduced as an important figure, such as the hero's best friend or brother, and then vanishes in the second act, this will be perceived as a glaring flaw in the script. In most cases this character should be cut from the script and their lines and action given to someone who sticks around. If the character *is* necessary to the story, then work to weave them into the action throughout the script.

If one of these key characters doesn't show up until Act Two, you may have to go back and set them up in the first act, at least in dialogue, depending on how significant they are to the protagonist and the plot. However, beware of characters who pop up out of nowhere to solve a problem or provide a convenient bit of information. For instance, if the hero gets fired in the second act, we need to see the boss *before* the boss gives the hero the axe. Setting up such characters early on makes their dramatic beats credible rather than contrived.

Insufficient character and relationship development: Developing the characters and their relationships is one of the biggest challenges in writing a screenplay. However, believable character growth is often what separates fair scripts from superior ones. Stories with characters who change significantly appeal to both actors and audiences, and they also give your story emotional depth.

It's usually not difficult to figure out how you want your character to change; the difficulty comes in finding a way to show this change bit by bit during the second act, instead of having the hero suddenly see the light and become brave or mature or empathetic in the last scene. One way to deal with this is to write an emotional outline, similar to your plot outline. In each sequence, determine where the character is in their growth. How do they feel about what's going on? Has the character changed at all yet? If so, how—and more importantly, why? The events your hero experiences in each sequence should have a specific effect on them. You can apply this technique to tracking how the relationships between the major players evolve over the course of the story.

Lack of complications: Video game developers make their games addicting by constantly increasing the tension and difficulty at each level of play. Slaying one dragon leads to a dozen more dragons charging towards you. Winning one race shifts your car into a higher gear and more obstacles are thrown in your path. Use this same approach with your story but translate it into dramatic and emotional terms.

A complication is different than an obstacle. An obstacle may be overcome without changing anything. A complication is the *result* of overcoming an obstacle, in which things are now worse than they were before. A character who desperately needs money asks for a raise—and ends up getting fired as a result. If the raise were just refused, then the character would remain in the same position as before. Getting fired makes their situation worse and triggers the need for a new course of action. This sort of complication is also known as a "reversal," because it reverses the path the character was on.

The formula for a compelling second act generally follows this formula: Every time things seem to be going well, they get worse; and every time things seem like they *can't* get any worse, they do. Do your best to continually increase the stakes for your hero. Make their goal harder and harder to solve, due mainly to the actions the hero takes. Ask yourself: 1) How can I increase the personal and/or emotional stakes?; 2) How can I make things more difficult for the protagonist?; 3) What new element can I introduce that will test the protagonist and/or force them to change in some way? Be sure that any complication you add emerges organically from the story and isn't a contrived twist that comes out of nowhere.

<u>The missing midpoint</u>: The midpoint of the script usually falls right where its name would imply: midway into your script. It is also where the biggest complication or reversal of the story usually occurs. If you think of your storyline like an arc, this moment is the peak. The set-up and its ensuing action build to this moment—even though it may sometimes be a low point for the character. Whether high or low, the midpoint defines what comes afterward. The midpoint may radically change the protagonist's circumstances and kick the story into a higher gear. Sometimes the lead's initial goal is solved; sometimes something happens that changes their goal substantially. In THE WIZARD OF OZ, Dorothy and her friends arrive in Oz and are admitted to see the Wizard. This goal has driven the film up to this point. However, instead of granting Dorothy's wish to go home, the Wizard insists she kill the Wicked Witch of the West first. Dorothy now has a new goal, which heightens the stakes and drives the ensuing action.

For more examples of complications and midpoint reversals see "Beyond the Premise: How to Develop a Compelling Story" in the Plot section.

<u>Failing to milk the climax</u>: The climax of your story, which comes at the end of the second act, is the high point of your script in terms of its impact on the audience (even though it's most likely the low point for your hero). Make sure you don't gloss over this key sequence. This is often one of the set pieces that your audience remembers most vividly, because it usually contains the most intense emotions and dramatic substance. Think of the scene in TOOTSIE where Dustin Hoffman reveals his true identity during a live taping of his soap opera.

The second act will no doubt take up the bulk of your rewriting efforts, and you may need several drafts to get it right. Even once you do, your work isn't done. The third act provides the final impact on your audience, and it requires care and attention, too. Read on for solutions to common third act problems.

THE THIRD ACT: GOING OUT WITH A BANG

A strong third act can make the difference between a pass and a recommend from a reader. A story analyst who's leaning towards passing can be won over by a powerful resolution that makes earlier problems seem less daunting to fix. Conversely, a reader who is on the fence will be put off by weak, corny, or contrived final scenes. The problems listed below are some of those often found in scripts that did not make the grade:

Unresolved subplots: As with the magical disappearing characters mentioned in the last chapter, writers sometimes introduce subplots in the first or second acts that ultimately aren't as necessary as the writer initially thought. This is fine for a first draft. However, in rewriting, it's important to home in on the important throughlines and cut the extraneous ones. Often these "lost" subplots have to do with the personal backstory of the protagonist and don't have an integral connection to the action of the plot. Subplots that are underdeveloped yet essential to the plot need to be woven in throughout the script and resolved either by the end of the second act or in the third act. If a component from the protagonist's personal backstory is significant, such as a female cop's battle with her ex-husband over child support, for instance, find a way for this issue to impact the cop's ability to deal with her job throughout the script, or have an effect on some other aspect of the plot.

No character arc: A character arc is an important part of a dramatic story, which is why I devote an entire essay to it in this book. The best screenplays revolve around characters who are changed by the experiences they undergo during the course of the plot. Most successful films have a lead character who transforms in some way. Characters who evolve are more emotionally compelling, and they give a film story more resonance and meaning: the audience feels that they, like the character, have learned something by the end. As mentioned in the earlier essay, the arc doesn't need to be for the better. A naive character may turn cynical; an honorable man may end up corrupt.

Sudden or unbelievable character arcs: While character arcs are important, writers often try to tag them on at the very end. A bully suddenly realizes the error of his ways in the last scene. The guy who can't commit suddenly realizes he loves his girlfriend and wants to marry her. However, in order for the change to be believable and satisfying, the writer needs to build up to it throughout the story. In terms of the leads' transformations, every sequence of the second act should have an effect on them and take them one step closer to their ultimate transformation. This way, the final step in their journey will feel inevitable rather than forced. Not *every* notable character needs to see the light, however. Some people aren't redeemable—or, conversely, corruptible—and it's fine to leave some of the supporting players as the same people they were at the start.

Deus ex machina: This term comes from Greek plays, in which the actor playing a god would literally be lowered down from above to save the day. This convenient solution to a dramatic situation or crisis was acceptable in ancient times, but today it comes across like a cheat. A "deus ex machina" doesn't need to be a literal person; it can simply be an overly contrived, easy solution. A killer can't suddenly confess simply because a cop has confronted them. No character should suddenly win the lottery or inherit a fortune at the end to solve their money problems, unless the possibility for this event has been credibly set up earlier.

In order for an ending to be satisfying—and more important, powerful—it needs to be earned. This requires conflict, tension, and characters who overcome extreme obstacles in order to achieve the goals they're striving for. The more difficult the solution is to come by, the greater the tension and the more moved your reader and later your audience will be.

V. <u>PLOT</u>

The essays in this section have been organized in no specific order. They each address either a concept that will help raise your plot above the ordinary, or address plot-related problems I've often found in scripts that prevented those scripts from excelling despite the screenplay's potential.

You can definitely jump around in reading these, or read them straight through and then come back to the ones that most apply to the script you're currently working on. You'll find a lot of overlap among these, as well as overlap with earlier essays. As I mentioned in the Introduction, if you see something repeated, it's because it's a common problem that turns up again and again; these essays are attempts to address these problems in more detail or come at them from a different angle.

SITUATION VS. STORY
TWIST VS. COMPLICATION
ELEMENTS OF A SCENE
CAUSE AND EFFECT
PLANTS AND PAYOFFS
WHEN TO LET YOUR AUDIENCE IN ON THE SECRET
HOW TO INCREASE THE TENSION
HOW TO INCREASE THE CONFLICT

SITUATION VS. STORY

One of the biggest challenges in developing a screenplay is finding a way to turn the dramatic situation you've come up with into a narrative story. This is similar to moving beyond the premise, discussed in the "Before You Begin" section. However, often writers will succeed in finding ways to complicate the set-up yet still fail to get the plot moving. I've already addressed some of these points in the essay on second act problems in the Structure section, as well as in a few essays in the Characterization section.

The main reason why scripts get stuck in situation mode is that the protagonist lacks a goal. The lead may find themselves in a predicament, and this predicament simply plays out over and over again with variations. The character may react to events, and things may even get worse, yet the script curiously lacks momentum. In order for the story to move forward, the central character has to *want* something specific. This objective should be established by the end of the first act at the latest. The protagonist then needs to actively pursue this goal, while encountering obstacles that make the goal more elusive and the character's predicament more difficult and/or complicated. Without a goal, the protagonist will seem reactive or even passive. Events occur *to* the protagonist, but these events are caused by other characters, instead of the protagonist's actions instigating the events. (See "Act Not React" in the Characterization section.) It's difficult to become engaged by such a character or know what we are supposed to root for.

A character's goal doesn't need to be overwhelmingly exciting, however. Not every story is a quest for a Holy Grail. You may even have a character whose objective is that they want things to stay the same, or they want to do nothing, even though the forces around them are trying to get them to act. However, such a person is not passive. They should be actively trying to maintain a status quo, with increasing difficulty.

Another reason why a story doesn't advance is because the character doesn't change, as discussed "Character Arc." The protagonist may have a goal, yet their pursuit of it fails to affect them in any notable way. As a result, although the action propels forward, the story seems to stand still. Every obstacle the protagonist encounters should lead to a choice. The decision the character makes to follow one path instead of another will demonstrate how they're changing due to their experiences. As the complications set in, and the obstacles become greater, these increasingly difficult choices will test the protagonist. Again, if you have a character who is resisting change, you still need to have *something* be changing in their lives, whether it's their circumstances or their relationships—or show how the character *is* changing, despite their goal not to.

For characters like superheroes, as mentioned in the "Character Arc" essay, even though the lead may not be going through a significant inner emotional journey, we should still ideally see some forward momentum in their characters: in how the increasing stakes and complications acting against them push them to do things they may not have thought of, for example, or been capable of at the beginning of the film.

We also need to see how external complications and personal choices lead a protagonist to a crisis point, which is where the character faces the biggest choice and the greatest obstacles. The character's response to this crisis leads to the resolution, which demonstrates how the events of the entire story have changed the character, and also makes clear how the character's actions and choices have led to this specific conclusion for the character's journey.

The journey is your story. The situation merely establishes the conflicting forces operating on your character during this journey. Make sure that your protagonist acts and changes due to these forces. The result will be a compelling screenplay rather than just a promising idea.

TWIST VS. COMPLICATION

Very often the roadblocks you face while writing your script are due to the slackening of tension in your story. Because the suspense has faded, you're not compelled to move forward. One way to heighten the tension is to add complications.

Writers often confuse the terms "twist" and "complication." Both are important elements of dramatic storytelling, but they usually perform different functions. A complication is a form of a twist, but a twist is not always a complication.

Pure twists can provide some good moments of shock and surprise in a script. Twists may end a movie on a startling and unexpected note, as was the case with THE USUAL SUSPECTS and THE SIXTH SENSE. In LES DIABOLIQUES and SLEUTH, twists are the core action, as characters whom we thought were dead suddenly turn up alive. While these twists do advance the plot, they don't complicate it. The main tension remains essentially the same.

Surprising a modern audience is difficult, however, because moviegoers and TV-viewers are more sophisticated now, and therefore familiar with practically every twist possible, thanks to the proliferation of clever crime shows and complex personal dramas. But making a surprise come out of nowhere is not the answer. If the twist is too far-fetched, it'll come across as infuriating and false. The best surprises are preceded by subtle hints that lead to an audience thinking "aha!" or "wow!" rather than "Oh, come on." These films also concentrate on character over plot. The audience is too engrossed in the protagonist's situation to be thinking ahead about the plot. THE CRYING GAME and THE SIXTH SENSE are examples of movies that follow these rules and therefore contain twists that truly surprise yet don't feel contrived.

Complications are more complex. Complications raise the stakes and/or take the plot in an entirely new direction. While a twist can often be seen coming or may be obvious in retrospect, a complication is a richer development in the story. The audience's response to a twist is: "Oh!" but the response to a complication is: "Oh, *no*."

The main complications in a script usually come at the end of the first and second acts, and are what propel the action into the following act. Classic genre movies offer familiar, often predictable complications, but they're good to study to help you identify the concept of the complication. For instance, in a standard romantic comedy, the two leads are often forced together in some way at the end of the first act. After they inevitably fall in love, they're separated at the end of the second act. A stock thriller may find the protagonist wrongly accused of murder at the end of the first act, for instance. At the end of the second, the hero discovers the true killer, who just happens to be the hero's wife, or boss, or best friend. In both genre examples, the complication changes the protagonist's situation completely.

Any type of story can have several smaller, subtler complications throughout the script, however. What all complications have in common is that they always make the protagonist's life more difficult.

TOOTSIE is a movie filled with clever complications. Dustin Hoffman's character's struggle to keep his identity as a man in drag a secret is complicated not only by his crush on Jessica Lange's character, but also by the crushes two male characters develop on his female persona. When his best friend, played by Teri Garr, catches him trying on her clothes, he distracts her by seducing her and complicates his life even further. His success as "Dorothy" also leads to his acting contract being renewed, thereby trapping him in a dress seemingly forever. In response to each of these complications, Hoffman's character has to continually revise his plan of attack, and this makes the action increasingly involving, tense, funny, and surprising.

Because your characters are forced to react and change in order to tackle these unexpected obstacles to their goals, complications add dimension to the characterizations, as well as to the plot, thereby preventing your story from being one-note and predictable.

ELEMENTS OF A SCENE

Once you've completed a couple of drafts of your script and feel you have the structure pretty much in place, it's time to zoom in and analyze individual scenes. You'll inevitably find a few scenes you feel are important to the story in terms of character or plot development, but which lack the excitement and/or tension of the scenes you know *are* working.

To develop these troubled scenes to their potential, make sure they contain one or more of the following qualities:

1. <u>Someone wants something, and there's an obstacle to them getting it</u>. Not every scene can or should be a bloody battle for survival. However, you'll add momentum and tension if the main character of the scene wants something, even if it's a snack to ease a hunger pang or a cab to get to work on time. If you have an expository beat, try making it take place while the character is trying to achieve some simple physical goal. You'll be amazed at the increased energy level of the scene. Characters can also have less tangible goals, such as wanting to be understood, wanting sympathy, or wanting to get a rise out of someone—all of which will add drama to an ordinary action or conversation.

2. <u>The scene can be summed up as either a chase or an escape</u>. There are two possible motivations in a scene: chase or escape. A character is either pursuing something or fleeing something. This "something" can be physical or emotional in nature. A subtler way to define this concept is that a character is either hoping for something (chase) or fearing something (escape). Figuring out which of these two categories your scene falls into will help you clarify and focus the action.

3. <u>The scene moves the main character forward</u>. Again, this can happen emotionally or physically. For example, the action can have an emotional or psychological effect on the character and cause some kind of inner change, so that at the end of the scene, they're a different person than they were at the beginning. Alternatively, the scene can bring the character closer to their goal, or put an obstacle in their path that pushes them further away from their goal. The latter is technically a step *backward*, but it still creates momentum in terms of the character's movement in the story; the obstacle compels the protagonist to try a new tactic or change direction in their quest to achieve their goal. The key plot points in your story should ideally propel the main character both emotionally *and* physically.

4. <u>The scene has a structure</u>. If your scene contains the above three elements, it will inherently have a structure: a beginning, middle, and end. The beginning makes the situation or problem clear. What does the character want? What are they hoping for or fearing? The middle intensifies the situation, presenting obstacles, complications, and/or resistance. The ending resolves the situation; the character either does or doesn't achieve their objective for the scene, and they and/or their path in the story has changed as a result.

5. <u>The scene has texture</u>. Ideally, a scene should accomplish more than one thing. One way to add texture or depth to a scene is to combine two scenes into one. For instance, if you have one scene where a character is making a phone call in order to get some key information, and another where they're eluding the villain, combining the two will instantly add dimension. Now the exposition scene has suspense: Can the protagonist complete the call without getting caught? In addition, the flight from the villain is made more difficult by the character's need to make the call. The new scene would end up as both a chase *and* an escape, but the two qualities would complement each other, heightening the excitement level as well as speeding up the pace of the action.

It's also a good idea to add physical texture to a scene wherever possible. What's the weather like? Would rain make the scene more difficult and therefore more interesting and dramatic? Does the geography of the location play off the essence or tone of the scene? Perhaps a cramped apartment would be a better setting for a confrontation than a deserted road. How does the time of day affect the action? Does sound play a part? What's interesting, unusual, or unique about the clothing the characters are wearing? Are there objects in the location that can be used in the scene for dramatic purposes? Don't overload a scene with too many of these elements, or the point of the action will be lost, but one or two interesting details can make the difference between a memorable scene and a forgettable one.

An activity can also add texture. A conversation could take place during a darts game, or while one character is washing the dishes. Ideally, any activity should tie in thematically with the main action of the scene.

6. <u>The action and dialogue are not on the nose</u>. Subtlety and subtext will get you a lot further than melodrama and relying on the obvious. It's much more involving to watch characters trying to avoid telling the truth than to passively observe them as they willingly reveal everything. Finding a way to have a character express love, hate, anger, or joy by means of contrary action or indirection is more challenging for the writer but more rewarding for the reader and/or audience, because this is where true creativity really shines. You can get as much information across with a lie as with the truth, but the lie has more art to it.

7. <u>There's some kind of time pressure</u>. This doesn't have to be as dramatic as a ticking bomb, but there should be a logical beginning and ending point in time for the scene. If the scene could potentially go on endlessly, this dissipates its sense of urgency and importance. You can add a time constraint simply by shifting the location of a scene. For instance, one character could be waiting for a train or be late for a meeting.

8. <u>There's friction in the scene</u>. Anything you can do to make the scene more difficult for the characters involved will raise the stakes and increase the tension. Friction can take many forms: characters with opposing goals; physical or emotional obstacles for the main character of the scene; reluctance or resistance of some kind on the part of the character; difficulty created by the environment, etc. It can even come via a character's misperception—seeing friction that's not really there. For example, near the end of LOVE AFFAIR (the movie on which AN AFFAIR TO REMEMBER was based), Charles Boyer pays a call on Irene Dunne. He wants to sit next to her on the sofa, but she doesn't move her legs to give him room. *We* know this is because she is crippled, but Boyer believes she's hinting that she wants him to leave. The simple dialogue of the scene therefore contains considerable tension, as we root for Boyer to figure out the truth, while also fearing he will grow so uncomfortable that he'll finally walk out, ending their relationship forever.

9. <u>There's comedy in the scene</u>. This doesn't need to be true for all scenes, of course, but if you have a scene that seems too dry, try adding a comic moment of some kind. This can be a bit of witty dialogue, a wry observation, or an odd, unexpected obstacle or twist. Dramas benefit from humor as much as comedies do. Even the most tragic events in life are often peppered with moments of irony.

10. <u>**The scene has a triangle in it**</u>. Again, this isn't necessary for every scene, but if the tension is sagging, adding a third point in an interchange between two characters increases the tension. This third point may be a character or an object. A third character can create trouble by taking one person's side over the other, or simply by being in the way, making it more difficult for the interaction between the two central characters to proceed. An object could be a physical obstacle for one or both characters, or it could be something that binds the characters together against their will. In ON THE WATERFRONT, Marlon Brando is trying to woo the reluctant Eva Marie Saint during a conversation in a park. In order to keep her as a captive audience, he picks up one of her gloves; she can't leave until she gets the glove back from him. This makes the scene infinitely more tense and interesting than it would have been if they'd just sat down and talked.

Many of these scene elements overlap; the common denominator for all of them is that they give the scene an extra dimension, usually by increasing the tension. The richer your individual scenes are, the stronger your screenplay will be overall.

CAUSE AND EFFECT

Without a strong sense of cause and effect, your story will come across like a contrived collection of random scenes. Every event, character, and object you introduce in your screenplay should have an effect on what happens in the ensuing scenes. This will make the action credible, logical, compelling, and complex. Scripts with strong cause and effect are impossible to put down, and they keep an executive or story analyst reading eagerly right up to the end.

Cause and effect is more than just one scene leading to the next. Anything that happens in a script needs to be carried through to its endpoint. Often a writer will include an event in a script in order to get a character into a certain situation, but then never refer to the event again. For instance, a script may begin with a published exposé written by the protagonist, which leads to the protagonist engaged with villains in a dangerous battle for survival. However, once the battle begins, the exposé is forgotten. We never find out how the protagonist even knew about the scandal, and there are no outside ramifications for any of the peripheral people involved. This ultimately renders the set-up unbelievable and forced.

When cause and effect are used properly, they can create considerable tension in a story, as the events snowball, generating greater and greater problems for the main character. In THE APARTMENT, Shirley MacLaine is an elevator operator having an affair with a married executive. At an office party, the executive's drunken secretary reveals to MacLaine that she too had an affair with the executive, as have several other women in the company. This conversation leads to MacLaine attempting suicide in Jack Lemmon's apartment, where she and her lover had been meeting. In many scripts, this would have been as far as the cause and effect would go, since the two leads have now been thrown together. However, screenwriters Billy Wilder and I.A.L. Diamond exploit the ramifications of the party scene to their maximum potential. The executive, annoyed with his secretary for putting a crimp in his love life, fires her. As a result, the secretary calls the executive's wife and tells her about her husband's philandering. The wife files for divorce, leading the executive to propose to MacLaine, which undermines the romantic aspirations of Lemmon, who has fallen in love with MacLaine. One thing leads inevitably to another in a richly woven narrative tapestry. The writers didn't need to contrive any external obstacles or complications, because by simply playing out the effects of the early events, the conflict naturally builds. If just one story thread of this plot was removed, the entire script would unravel.

Even minor events in a story need to have ramifications. For example, if a character gets into a fight in one scene, they should have bruises in the next scene and other characters should comment on them. This not only helps the logic of your plot but also adds texture to it. In THE APARTMENT, Jack Lemmon spends a winter night locked out of his apartment. As a result, he gets a cold, the symptoms of which are used as gags in the ensuing scenes.

Any scene you can remove from your script without changing anything that comes before or after is extraneous and not organic to your story. To make it organic, try to find a way to tie the action into the overall plot by having the scene be a clear result of something that happened earlier and/or lead to something that happens later. In this way, your narrative becomes a tightly structured and complex whole, rather than a loosely assembled assortment of arbitrary parts.

The concept of cause and effect can also be seen in the smaller plot details of a screenplay: plants and payoffs. I'll discuss these in more detail in the next essay.

PLANTS AND PAYOFFS

Plants and payoffs can give your script depth and breadth, but they require deft handling or else your plot will come off as artificial. This is why looking for ways to set up later events or revelations, or finding ways to carry certain motifs, objects, or lines of dialogue through your script, is usually tackled in revision, not in a first draft. You want your plants and payoffs to seem to emerge naturally from your story, rather than come off as "clever tricks" foisted onto the characters and the plot by the writer.

What are plants and payoffs? A simple way to explain is with a familiar axiom: if you show a gun in an early scene (plant), it had better go off at a later point (payoff). If it doesn't, the audience will feel cheated, and your story will seem like it's missing something. Conversely, if a gun is to go off at some point, then we better have seen the gun earlier on in the story. Otherwise the later action will come across as contrived.

Plants and payoffs come in all shapes and forms. Writer/director Billy Wilder was a master at this technique. Studying any of his films will give you hundreds of examples of plants and payoffs to examine. As a test case, let's look again at the plot of THE APARTMENT, which boasts an elegant cohesiveness via the use of plants and payoffs. Every character has a unique way of speaking, and certain phrases common to one character are often mimicked later by other characters. For instance, one of the executives that Jack Lemmon's character works with, played by David Lewis, likes to add "-wise" to the end of everything: "Premium-wise and billing-wise, we're eighteen percent ahead of last year, October-wise." Later, when Shirley MacLaine's character laments her inability to fall in love with a nice guy like Lemmon, he responds, "That's the way it crumbles, cookie-wise." MacLaine then uses this exact phrase when she dumps her lover, played by

Fred MacMurray. The replay of these phrases pulls the audience into the story. Just as we come up with catch phrases with our friends, when movie characters do the same, it makes the world you've created feel familiar and authentic. Wilder also uses props for payoffs in the movie. Lemmon takes a sleeping pill at the beginning of the movie (plant) and MacLaine later overdoses on the same pills (payoff). Lewis's character forgets his champagne after Lemmon refuses to let him bring his girlfriend into the apartment in a second act scene, and later, in the third act, Lemmon opens the champagne on New Year's Eve. MacLaine, arriving outside his apartment, hears the pop and thinks Lemmon has shot himself. This beat pays off the plant of the champagne as well as an earlier plant: when Lemmon told MacLaine he once tried to shoot himself over an unrequited love. Because we've been filled in earlier on the characters' backstories, these payoffs make us feel like insiders in the action.

As mentioned, the potential for both plants and payoffs is best determined in rewrites. Every revision will reveal a new opportunity for you to set up an important dramatic beat earlier in the script or pay off on a line of dialogue later. For instance, it's possible Wilder and his co-writer I.A.L. Diamond added the scene of Lemmon taking the sleeping pill in a later draft, in order to plant the pills.

Consider these tips when dealing with this technique:

1. **Beware the obvious set-up**. Say you have a mantel clock that will blow up at some point, as a surprise. Don't have a character suddenly point to the clock for no reason in the middle of an early scene. Make sure the reference to the clock is essential to the early scene in some way. This way, we'll register that the clock exists without wondering why in the world the character has pointed it out.

2. **<u>Don't overdo the dialogue payoffs</u>**. There's a fine line between the realistic repeating of catch phrases, and arch, theatrical speech. Put less effort into being clever and more into making the characters sound like real people. Payoffs in dialogue work best when they're used primarily for key dramatic moments.

3. **<u>Streamline</u>**. For example, if an old LP record ends up having a significant emotional meaning for the story or a character, yet we also learn at some point about another object with similar personal import, such as a book of poetry, eliminate one of these. This makes the role of the remaining single object much stronger and more resonant.

4. **<u>Consider the genre</u>**. Plants and payoffs work well in comedy, where the repetition of actions or phrases can be used for humor. In more serious stories, they need to be used much more subtly and sparingly. Nevertheless, meaningful catch phrases in a character drama or a clever payoff on a planted prop or event in a suspense film can be very effective if done well. Just be careful not to go overboard or else the action will start to seem coy rather than clever.

5. **<u>It doesn't have to be obvious</u>**. Plants and payoffs are often so indirect and understated that they only become apparent on repeated viewings of a film. However, they're still working, on a subconscious level, to create a contained, three-dimensional world for your story.

The technique of plants and payoffs is an important element of the screenwriting craft, but one that takes practice to carry off well. Studying other films will help you see how professional screenwriters use this device to give texture and life to their stories.

WHEN TO LET YOUR AUDIENCE IN ON THE SECRET

Predictability is something every writer wants to avoid. This doesn't mean every beat of your script needs to be a surprise, however. There are times when letting your audience in on the secret will actually improve your story.

Alfred Hitchcock once offered this description to demonstrate the difference between surprise and suspense: Two people sit at a café table, unaware that there is a bomb ticking beneath it. The audience doesn't know about the bomb = surprise. The audience *does* know = suspense.

Though surprises provide shock value, suspense carries much more dramatic weight. For instance, in CHARADE, the audience is shown early on that Cary Grant's character is in cahoots with the three villains who want the fortune hidden by Audrey Hepburn's late husband. By letting us in on this information, the filmmakers create several layers of tension: 1) we wonder when Hepburn's character will find out the truth; 2) we worry for her safety; and 3) we wonder what Grant's true agenda is.

In THE MANCHURIAN CANDIDATE, neither Laurence Harvey's character nor any of the people closest to him (with one notable exception) is aware that Harvey has been brainwashed into becoming an assassin. The audience knows practically from the start, however, and this makes every beat of the movie fraught with tension as we wait for disaster to strike.

Of course, there's no reason why the information the writer presents to the audience needs to be true. Audiences love to be tricked, if the trick is handled cleverly. One of the most well-known instances of this is in THE USUAL SUSPECTS, in which the filmmakers shift suspicion from one character to the next, only to have any assumptions the audience has made shattered by the final revelation of the movie. Similarly, in murder mysteries like AND THEN THERE WERE NONE (along with its many remakes and imitators), the mostly likely suspects are systematically killed off until the audience is sure they know whodunit—or do they? In CHARADE, when Audrey Hepburn learns Cary Grant has been lying to her, he *seems* to come clean—yet his new story later turns out to be a lie as well. This happens again and again, to the point where neither Hepburn's character nor we know what to believe.

A more subtle form of early revelation is foreshadowing. While this technique doesn't clearly reveal information, it helps prepare your audience subconsciously for later events. In THE BRIDGE ON THE RIVER KWAI, the movie opens with William Holden and a fellow prisoner burying the last of the POWs with whom they had served time at their camp in the Pacific. This graveyard is shown throughout the movie, often in the background of scenes, subtly hinting at the tragedy that is to come.

Plots in which every dramatic beat is a shock or surprise aren't involving, they're contrived. There's a fine line between telling an audience too little and telling them too much. It's worth analyzing your script in detail in order to keep as close to that line as possible. It can mean the difference between a simplistic, cartoony plot, and a rich, sophisticated, and dramatic story.

HOW TO INCREASE THE TENSION

The key to keeping a reader or audience riveted by your plot is to make sure the action is tense. Events that unfold easily and scenes that offer little beyond information are far from the stuff of gripping drama. Here are some suggestions for hiking up the tension in your screenplay:

1. **<u>A ticking clock</u>.** This can be as momentous as the hero's desperate need to escape from a locked room before a bomb explodes or as minor as a parent trying to get their child dressed before the school bus comes. In either case, there's pressure on a character to achieve their goal before the time is up, and this in turn adds tension.

2. **<u>Rush</u>**. Have one character in the scene be in a hurry, but due to a more general time pressure than the ticking clock. For example, if the hero is trying to apologize to their girlfriend while she's scrambling to get ready for work, then this conversation is a lot more difficult than if it took place over a relaxed breakfast. The tension in this type of scene tends to be more emotional or mental than physical.

3. **<u>A ticking bomb</u>**. Unlike the metaphorical ticking clock, where the characters are aware of the time pressure, a metaphorical ticking bomb is something known only to the audience (as discussed in the previous essay.) If we see a gangster plant a bomb in a car, or know the villain is hiding around the corner, this creates suspense as we wait for the truth to be discovered before it's too late. Again, this concept can apply to any genre of film, not just thrillers. For instance, in a romantic comedy, we might learn that the person whom the lead has fallen for is dating the lead's best friend, but neither the lead, their romantic interest, nor the best friend knows. We then wait, tensely, for when one of the members of the triangle finds out. If

whomever learns the truth keeps it a secret, the tension would then shift to wondering when the others will discover what's going on—and to what will happen as a result.

4. **A necessary trade-off**. If a character has to sacrifice something by committing an act, this adds tension to their decision process and to the action. The classic example of this is the hostage situation in a crime drama. Does the hero shoot and risk killing the hostage, or not shoot and chance letting the villain get away? Another familiar example is in relationship stories where the hero is about to declare their love for the love interest—just as they learn their love interest loves someone else. Does the lead risk humiliation by stating their feelings anyway? Or do they sacrifice their own happiness by keeping mum?

5. **Mystery**. Think of the protagonist venturing down a dark corridor or the detective peering into a sinister alley. When a character pursues a course of action to which the outcome is uncertain, this creates a sense of unease in the audience, which translates to tension.

6. **Difficulty speaking**. This can be either emotional or physical. Someone may be so grief-stricken, angry, or embarrassed that speech is nearly impossible, or two characters may have to whisper in order to prevent being overheard. In either case, the difficulty presented by the situation increases the tension in what would otherwise be just an average conversation.

7. **Reversal of expectations (for the worse)**. If the result of a character's actions leads to the opposite of what they hoped for, this creates tension, as we wonder what they will do next. For instance, a man may propose to his long-time girlfriend, only to have her turn him down. What does he do now? This device is often used to create comic tension. In MEET THE

PARENTS, for instance, every attempt by Ben Stiller to fix the problems he's caused results in a worse situation and escalates the tension in the film. (See "Twist vs. Complication" for more examples.)

8. **A Challenging Environment**. The addition of an external element will often increase the tension in a script. Thunderstorms make the completion of an outdoor activity more challenging than sunshine would, for example. A city with narrow, crowded streets results in a tenser chase scene than a pursuit down an empty highway. A large, darkened, and decrepit house is spookier than a cozy, sunny cottage. A dinner scene where the hero is surrounded by hostile in-laws is a lot tenser than a party with old friends.

9. **Things are going too well**. Ironically, tension can arise during a scene or sequence in which everything seems to be going perfectly. The key word here is "seems." Audiences are attuned to the basic rules of drama and know that when things are going too well, it generally means this is merely the calm before the storm. If the two romantic leads happily hook up halfway into the movie, we know some monkey wrench to their relationship is around the corner. If the cop catches the villain early on in the film, we recognize that this is not the end of the story, and we wait tensely for the other shoe to drop.

10. **Increase in conflict**. Heightening the conflict is one of the most fundamental ways to add tension to a scene or sequence. There are many ways to increase conflict, and I'll discuss some of them in the next essay.

HOW TO INCREASE THE CONFLICT

As mentioned above, one of the best ways to increase the tension in your script is to increase the conflict. Conflict can come from many different sources:

1. **Opposing Goals**. This is the most common and most fundamental type of interpersonal conflict. One character wants one thing, while the other character wants the opposite, and a battle (physical and/or verbal) ensues. The fight could be over an object, a person, or even an idea. This type of conflict should be present in some form in every major scene, even if it's in the subtext of the characters' interactions.

2. **Misunderstanding**. Misinterpretations of actions or words, mistaken identity, and missed connections are all fundamental elements of most comedies. In BRIDGET JONES' DIARY, we know that Colin Firth's Mark Darcy character likes Bridget, played by Renee Zellweger, but she continually misinterprets his comments as slights. This creates discomfort and therefore tension in nearly every scene that Zellweger and Firth have together. Misunderstandings can fuel more serious stories as well. For instance, in a suspense film, a man might be wrongly suspected of being someone else, and the misunderstanding results in him being hunted by both criminals and the police.

3. **Betrayal**. The lover who cheats on their spouse, the work colleague who claims credit for the hero's idea, the criminal who rats on their partner, the friend who betrays the hero's secret—these are all examples of traitorous behavior. These situations create conflict between the characters involved and intensify the drama in any story.

4. **Deception**. A close relative of betrayal, deception is when a character is untruthful, whether it's about an affair, a secret from their past, a crime, or even good news that the protagonist desires to keep to themselves for some reason. Conflict arises when the deceiver works to prevent other characters from discovering the truth.

5. **Character transformation**. This can be a physical transformation, such as Jim Carrey's metamorphosis from a meek bank clerk to a partying madman in THE MASK, or a less spectacular but just as dramatic emotional transformation, as in WORKING GIRL, when Melanie Griffith develops self-confidence while posing as her boss and becomes more assertive as a result. In both cases, the character's change causes friction with the world and people around them.

6. **Unexpected traits**. Here a character doesn't change but instead reveals skills or knowledge not previously visible. For instance, Anne Hathaway's discovery of her inner "material girl" in THE DEVIL WORE PRADA creates conflict in her relationships with her friends and boyfriend, and intensifies her rivalry with her fellow assistant.

7. **A character tries to push another character beyond their capabilities**. This is the classic conflict in the buddy movie formula and sometimes shows up in romantic comedies as well. Two opposites are thrown together and one or both tries to force the other to conform to their attitude toward the world. The resistance of one or both to changing creates conflict between them, which often spills over into the action. For example, if they have to team up to achieve a specific goal in a scene, their personal battle will likely make achieving this goal more difficult.

8. **Information withheld**. This could fall under "opposing goals," as when a cop is grilling a subject but the subject refuses to answer the cop's questions. However, a protagonist may also be seeking information from a source other than a human being. There have been many films where a character attempts to solve a puzzle or break a spell; the obstacles they face in pursuing this knowledge creates suspense.

9. **Inner conflict**. Conflict isn't always manifested externally as a battle between the protagonist and antagonist or other opposing force. Conflict may also involve just the character alone. The protagonist may feel a moral resistance to an action they're being asked or compelled to carry out. A character may also be out of their emotional or mental depth when attempting to solve a problem. Insecurity, intellectual inferiority, and even physical limitations can cause a character to resist taking action. This internal conflict does need to be shown visually, however. The screenwriter must demonstrate, via dialogue and/or behavior, how and why the character is struggling inside.

10. **Lack of conflict**. Ironically, there are occasions where the absence of conflict can create conflict. This happens, for instance, when the protagonist attempts to engage another character and the other character refuses to be engaged. For example, a character may try to initiate a discussion with their spouse about their troubled relationship and the spouse ignores them. This escalates the tension in the scene, because we can sense the increasing hostility beneath the surface of both characters.

11. **A resolved problem recurs**. This could be thought of as "Part Two" of "Things are going too well" discussed in the previous essay. For example, in a romantic comedy, the hero may have vanquished their romantic rival and won over their love interest, only to have the rival reappear with a new

plan to woo the object of the hero's affection. In a crime drama, the cop's arrest of the criminal could be followed by either the criminal's escape or the perpetration of another crime that indicates the cop has arrested the wrong person.

Conflict and tension go hand in hand, and they're the key elements of any good screenplay. Without conflict there's no drama, and without tension it's impossible for a reader or viewer to become engaged by the film's story. For scenes in your script that seem flat or unfocused, try applying one or more of the suggestions in this or the previous essay. Once you've introduced some tension and/or conflict into the action, you'll be surprised by how the energy picks up. The result will be a screenplay that will grip agents and producers from the start, and, more importantly, keep them reading all the way to the last page of your screenplay.

VI. <u>REVISION</u>

As I discussed in the Introduction, the intent of this book is to help you identify and fix typical problems in characterization, structure, and plot, in order to make the script you have better. This is the essence of revision. However, a few of the essays I wrote over the years dealt with revision as a specific topic, and I've therefore placed them here, in their own section.

In the following essays, I focus first on a handful of issues that tend to crop up in first drafts and in scripts by first-time writers. I then offer advice on ways to tackle problems both big and small when you're revising. ("What is Coverage?" in the Bonus Content section also offers a few revision tips.)

You don't need to fix everything on the first revision. Trying to do this will only bring you frustration, which in turn may lead you to neglect problems that need to be addressed in order for your screenplay to reach its potential. Fix whatever you can, take a break, and then return to revise some more. As you move from draft to draft, the process will become easier because the remaining problems will be smaller. You'll feel more encouraged as you watch your final story emerge from that metaphorical block of clay.

COMMON PROBLEMS TO CONSIDER
REWRITING TACTICS: MACRO
REWRITING TACTICS: MICRO
HOW TO TAKE FEEDBACK
FINAL POLISH

COMMON PROBLEMS TO CONSIDER

Every screenplay is different and therefore its writer will have different challenges to tackle in revision. A character study may need work in the area of cause and effect, while an action story might have a protagonist that currently lacks depth and complexity. However, there are four issues that often crop up in rough drafts, no matter the genre:

1. <u>An overwritten beginning</u>. In early drafts of most written works, from novels to scripts to plays, the writer is often writing themselves "into the story": getting to know the characters, uncovering the interpersonal conflicts, establishing the dramatic situation, and building the world of the story. This results in an opening that's far too long. It's best not to fight this when you're writing the first draft because you want your subconscious to let everything out. However, once you move into the second draft, it's time to look hard at the early scenes in your first act. You may find you can condense or even cut the first ten to twenty pages of your script. By skipping ahead to the moment when the conflict really begins, you instantly create momentum and are likely to hook a reader much more quickly. This will also challenge you to find a way to get across important expository information about the characters and setting *as* the story is progressing. This in turn will add complexity to your scenes.

2. <u>Too much detail at the start; too little later</u>. Similarly, the initial few scenes of a first draft tend to be very detailed, while later scenes are more general and vague. This is usually because the writer has had more time with the early scenes, tweaking them a bit during each writing session. Detail is important, because it creates texture and depth. However, there are often plot points or character aspects that are given a big build-up at the start and then end up having no importance later in the story. In rewriting, narrow in on and strengthen only those elements that play a part through-out the whole script, and cut down or cut out the rest. Then be sure to flesh out the later scenes so they're as rich as the revised opening ones.

3. The theme has not yet been set up. As discussed in the "Theme" essay, the true meaning of the script often doesn't make itself clear until the writer reaches the end of the rough draft. At this point, it's necessary to go back and reassess the first and second acts, in order to determine whether they match the story's ultimate meaning. For instance, you may have started with a story about a ballplayer trying to break into the majors but realized by the end that the story is actually about the ballplayer's need to win a parent's approval. In the revision, you'd want to make sure you've introduced the parent and this dramatic need in the first act—ideally in the first ten pages.

4. The personal throughline is unevenly developed. Many scripts begin by introducing interesting characters with intriguing personal problems, but then the personal aspect is forgotten as the plot takes over. Look hard at the second act and see if there are places where the dramatic events of the plot are so dominant that your protagonist's emotional journey gets lost. The action should always relate somehow to your character's growth.

Each new draft you write ideally peels back a layer of superficiality and cliché from your screenplay, leading you deeper into the story and characters, as well as bringing out your original voice. Don't be afraid to perform a major overhaul on sequences that aren't working, and don't neglect to change a scene just because it means others will have to change as a result. Rewriting is hard work, but the more effort you put in, the better your script will be and the greater your chance for success.

REWRITING TACTICS: MACRO

You've finished a draft, you've read it through, and you're ready to make those major changes you know you need. But when you begin to rewrite, you find yourself unable to do little more than move some scenes around, add a beat here and there, and finesse the dialogue. You know you need more than a polish, but the changes feel overwhelming and you fear they'll cause the whole thing to collapse. What can you do? Here are some suggestions:

1. **Start over.** If you put your first draft aside and start with a blank piece of paper (or blank screen), you'll be surprised how much this frees you up. Begin by writing an outline, as if you were starting your story from scratch. Add new scenes and make changes according to your notes, but don't refer to your original. You'll find that unnecessary scenes, sequences, and even characters will start to fall away because you'll only remember the parts of the script that really resonate with you. Use this new outline as a guideline for your rewrite.

2. **Plot the subplots separately**. To ensure you've developed every throughline to its potential, create a separate outline or timeline for each one. For example, plot out only the detective's search for the killer, from beginning to end. Then plot out the detective's relationship with their unstable spouse. Then plot out the killer's storyline, etc. By focusing on one subplot at a time, you can work on it as if it were the only plot, which will help you identify the weak points. Make sure you have a beginning, middle, and end to the subplot, and that all of the potential beats are present. Once you've developed each of the minor story threads sufficiently, go back and determine how you'll weave them together for maximum dramatic momentum and impact.

3. **Use index cards**. This is one of the most common suggestions made by screenwriting instructors and coaches, and for good reason. By taking the puzzle apart, you can look at it fresh and see how the pieces are really supposed to fit together (one index card per scene). This type of activity employs the analytical side of your brain. Once you determine the correct order of the scenes, you can get back to the creative work. (You can use index cards throughout the writing process, from brainstorm to polish. Whenever you hit a snag or run into some action that isn't working, step away from the script and use the index cards to work it out.)

4. **Work on separate sequences**. This is more worthwhile after you've employed any or all of the tactics above and have a clear idea of how you want your revised story to unfold. Sequences, like the script as a whole, have a beginning, middle, and end. They also have a structure: source of drama --> catalyst --> main question --> turning point --> resolution. If you work on sequences one at a time, you'll be able to strengthen and clarify this structure, and thereby increase the dramatic tension of both the sequence and your screenplay as a whole. You'll also end up with a plot that comes across as well-crafted rather than erratic. (See "Sequences: The Building Blocks of Your Script" in the Structure section for more on sequences.)

5. **Try different openings**. Although this suggestion deals with only a small part of the script, beginning your story on the right note can affect everything that comes after. The opening is also one of the easiest things to change, because you really can start a story anywhere. Set the first ten or so pages of your current draft aside and try any or all of these new versions: 1) Start the story later, as discussed in the previous essay. In other words, make the scene that occurs on page 11, or around page 11, the first scene of your script and go from there. 2) Do the same, but this time start on page 30. (This doesn't mean you'll lose everything from the first act, because

you may be able to find better ways to use some of the beats you cut later.) 3) Strike a completely different note. If the script now starts in action, for instance, open with a character scene instead. If the screenplay opens with a long dialogue scene, find a way to start the script in action, with very little dialogue. If the script begins with an exterior, try opening with an interior or even a close-up. If it starts inside, try setting it up with an exterior instead. 4) Focus on a different character in the opening scene. This sort of "play" can shake up your thinking and loosen the current draft's hold on you.

Be open-minded about trying major changes. You can always go back to what you had. (Make sure you save anything you cut in a separate document!) However, exploring other ways into a scene or event can unlock a key moment or beat you wouldn't have discovered otherwise. There can be a lot of sweat and tears involved in such a big revision, but the effort is worth it, because doing the work will help you bridge the gap between the good script you have and the *great* script it has the potential to be.

REWRITING TACTICS: MICRO

Once you've tackled the major issues in a revision, it's time to zero in on specific areas where there may still be problems. This type of revision is less overwhelming and more satisfying because you can often fix one or more of these problems in a single writing session. They are no less important, however. Demonstrating that you're a master of these smaller craft skills will show a reader or producer that you're a true professional.

Go through your script and ask yourself these questions:

1. **Is there a better place in the script to put any of the scenes or beats?** If there's a scene or moment (dramatic or emotional) in your script that you know is necessary but isn't quite gelling, trying looking for an alternative spot for it. Perhaps the protagonist's discovery of their brother's betrayal should come later or earlier, for instance, where it will have greater impact on the action. Maybe the robbery works better as the midpoint.

2. **Can you combine and/or condense any scenes or action within scenes?** A scene that's curiously static or lacking in energy may come to life by simply shrinking it down to its key points of conflict. Sometimes weaving a couple of closely occurring scenes together can have the same effect, by layering the drama of one of the scenes onto the other. In this latter case, you may find that once you've combined the scenes, you need to condense the result as well, to make it as tight—and involving—as possible.

3. **Can you cut any scenes out?** If you can take out a scene without affecting the story, then it's extraneous.

4. **Are there any scenes where the major character's goal in the scene is unclear or missing?** As discussed in earlier essays, characters' goals and the obstacles to those goals are what fuel the drama of your plot. If you don't know what the characters, especially the protagonist, want in the scene, you may not need the scene, or you may need to combine the key beats of the scene with another scene where the character's wants are clear —or you may need to revise the scene to clarify the goal.

5. **Does every action the character takes have a clear effect and/or ramification?** Look for scenes or series of beats where the protagonist isn't present or isn't active. If the action of the scene is unrelated to the protagonist, it's likely you don't need that scene, or else it needs to be rewritten to clarify how what is unfolding will affect the protagonist. The action may only affect them indirectly, although directly is ideal.

6. **Can you get to the heart of the scene more quickly?** This relates to some of the questions above, but it doesn't necessarily mean the scene is too long. Instead, it may be that you have a lot of lead-up to the true point of the scene, and then gloss over the point—rather than getting to it quickly and then spending sufficient time digging down more deeply. This is something to look at closely in key scenes especially.

HOW TO TAKE FEEDBACK

Getting constructive feedback on your screenplay is an essential step in rewriting, because giving your script to someone else to read will provide you with a fresh and objective point of view. In critique groups, classes, and workshops, writers often share pieces of a project as it's being developed and therefore the first piece of advice below may not apply. Whether you've written the script with the input of others or on your own, once you have a completed and fairly solid draft, it's worth seeking out an additional perspective from someone who has never seen the script, such as a trusted friend or script consultant.

In order to get the most from feedback, follow these tips:

1. **Don't give someone a half-finished script or one you know is seriously flawed**. This is a waste of both your time and your reader's, since they'll most likely pinpoint problems you already know exist. The criticism you receive when you don't yet have a solid hold on your story can also be damaging, causing you to doubt your idea and maybe even leading you to abandon the script altogether. The best time to solicit feedback is when you feel you've done everything you can: you know it's not perfect, but you don't know exactly what the remaining problems are.

2. **Do ask someone who will provide you with *constructive* critical feedback**. While it might give you a boost to have someone who is unconditionally supportive read your script and tell you it's brilliant, this shouldn't count as one of your official readers. Your goal isn't to get validation but to make your screenplay better. On the other hand, don't give your script to someone you know to be unfailingly negative, because such feedback is as useless as total praise.

3. **Do take notes**. If your feedback is verbal, do your best to write down everything that's said. It's hard to remember every detail when you're on the spot. Also, keeping notes forces you to focus on listening rather than instantly coming up with arguments for the reader's criticisms. If there are criticisms you don't agree with, note them, and come back to them at the end to discuss them in more detail and get clarification if necessary. If ideas on how to fix a problem come to you, write those down as well.

4. **Don't argue with the reader**. You've asked this person for their opinion, and an opinion, by definition, is neither right nor wrong. Don't try to convince your reader that their note is off-base or bully them into taking the comment back. You can, however, explain what you were trying to achieve. This can lead to a helpful discussion of how you fell short and what you can do to correct the problem.

5. **Do ask questions once you've heard all the notes**. Just because your reader failed to touch on a point that concerns you, don't assume this means it's not a problem. They may not have noticed it, or not thought it was worth mentioning, or they may not think it's a problem. The only way to know this is by asking. Also ask for clarification on any notes you don't understand or think you might have misunderstood. Your goal is to get as much information as you can.

6. **Don't take the feedback as gold**. Just as an opinion can't be wrong, it's also not necessarily right. However, do analyze the feedback closely. Although you may feel a solution proposed by your reader is inappropriate for the story, the reader's suggestion may still indicate a problem that is very real. In Hollywood terms, this is known as looking for "the note behind the note." Once you identify the true problem, you can come up with your own, more apt solution.

7. **<u>Do get more than one opinion</u>**. Ideally three readers will give you the benefit of different opinions while also underscoring the major problems; if two out of three or all three readers have the same note, this is probably a note you should take very seriously. If you give the script to more than three people, however, you'll start to get too many individual points of view, which is likely to confuse you and pull you in too many different directions.

8. **<u>Don't rewrite immediately</u>**. Give yourself a week or two to let the notes sink in. Your subconscious will help sort out the good from the bad. Often a writer will initially feel resistance to the notes that are the most on target. These comments tend to stick with the writer as they think about their story. The truly off-base notes, on the other hand, tend to be forgotten once it's time to rewrite.

When you return to revising, you may need to revisit the previous two essays in this section, as well as any earlier essays that relate to the problems your reader has identified and that you agree with. Once you've worked out all the major problems, and completed enough drafts that you feel the screenplay is near to perfect, you still need to go back for one final polish. You'll find tips on executing that polish in the next chapter.

FINAL POLISH

You're finished! After several drafts, you've ironed out all the plot glitches, you've developed the characters and their relationships to their potential, and you've milked the climax so that every beat is fraught with tension, leading to a powerful, unforgettable ending. You're ready to send the script out to agents and producers!

But wait—not so fast. These few final steps can make the difference between a flawed diamond and a polished gem.

1. **Examine each scene to determine if you can cut into it later or cut out of it earlier**. What happens if you cut the first two or three beats in the scene? Is the meaning of the scene still clear? Does the scene now have more energy? Cutting the last couple of lines and/or beats of action also might speed up the pace.

2. **Look for places to cut into dialogue or conversations later or cut out earlier**. Similar to the technique above, try cutting out the first and/or last dialogue exchange between characters in a scene. For monologues, see if you can cut the first and/or last sentence or two. One easy way to immediately sharpen the dialogue is to go through and cut out lead-in words like "Well," "But," and "Oh." These words can serve a purpose, but writers tend to overuse them and they can mute the impact of an important line. Also, cut any unnecessary parenthetical adjectives. Most of the time, the tone of the line is clear from the words themselves.

3. **Look for large chunks of description**. Busy readers and executives are likely to skip over long paragraphs and may miss important action as a result. If you have a paragraph of description that's over five or six lines long,

either cut it down or break it into separate paragraphs. The more "white space" you have on a page, the faster the script will move. You can also set off important moments of action by underlining, or using boldface or italics—just make sure you don't overuse this device or it will cease to help the words stand out.

4. **Read _just_ the dialogue aloud**. Because readers and executives often have several scripts to read a night, they may only read the dialogue once they get a sense of the story. For this reason, it's worth reading through your script once, reading only the dialogue. If any key beats are missing or unclear, consider indicating them in the dialogue—but only if the result won't sound forced. (Obviously, this wouldn't apply to pure action beats like battle scenes or car chases.)

5. **Read the whole script aloud to yourself**. Read both the description and the dialogue. This will help you catch dialogue that drags or trips up the tongue, as well as identify places where the rhythm of your writing gets tripped up by awkward phrasing. It can also help you notice repetitive phrases, and find typos spell check would miss, such as missing or misused words.

6. **Look for pages that are _all_ dialogue**. Dialogue-heavy scripts feel talky and/or stagy. If you have a scene of dialogue that goes on for more than a page, break it up with a few short lines of action, indicating what we're seeing on screen. What are the characters doing? How are they using their environment? Better yet, look for ways to cut the dialogue down. Do the characters repeat themselves? Do they make long-winded statements when one or two brief sentences will do? In general, unless a character is telling a story, no line of dialogue should be more than four or five lines on the page. If it is, it's likely that the meat of the message is either buried in the

middle of the speech or is in the last one or two sentences, and the rest is just filler. Remember that film is a visual medium. Memorable dialogue from films tends to be concise, directly to the point, and of key importance in the scene.

7. **ALWAYS perform a spell check and grammar check**. If there are words you often confuse (such as "its" and "it's") that a spellchecker might not always catch, perform a search for each of those words to make sure that you've used them correctly.

8. **Proofread**. A spell check won't catch everything, and a script filled with typos suggests the writer didn't care enough about their work to check for mistakes. You wouldn't give someone a hardcopy script covered with spaghetti sauce stains or that was missing pages, yet typos give an equally sloppy appearance. If you're someone who isn't detail-oriented, hire a proofreader or ask a detail-oriented friend to read through the script for you for one last check.

As you complete these tasks, you might find yourself tweaking your plot and characterizations here and there, which is a great side effect of this kind of final read-through. Your story will be smoother, sharper, and more professional as a result.

VII. <u>TROUBLESHOOTING</u>

The following three essays offer general advice on dealing with problems almost every screenwriter faces at some point while working on their current script, no matter what stage of the writing process they're in.

BLOCK BREAKERS
THE POWER OF LISTS
HOW TO COMMIT

BLOCK BREAKERS

The inability to sit down and face the page. The continuous need to take a nap. The certainty that the idea you came up with in the middle of last night is *definitely* a better concept for a screenplay than the one you're working on now. These are all signs you've hit a roadblock in your story. Giving up is always an option, but not a good one, because you're going to hit a roadblock on your next script, and the one after that. The only way to get past these roadblocks is to acquire the tools to break them down.

Here are a few exercises that act as dynamite to those roadblocks all writers face.

1. **The List.** A list can help at any stage of writing, from brainstorming to final polish. You simply make a long list of possible solutions to your problem—the longer the better. The ideal length of a list is too long to ever finish. For example, if a scene isn't working, write a list of twenty different directions the scene could go in. In addition to plowing through the clichés, the long list quiets the inner censor. Because the list must be long, you're forced to include the bad ideas, stupid ideas, trite ideas, and silly ideas. When you write down one of these bad or clichéd ideas, you get it out of your head. This allows you to gain access to your subconscious ideas: the more original choices that are unique to you. (I go into more detail on lists in the next essay.)

2. **The One-eighty.** You may find yourself endlessly polishing a certain scene over and over, moving commas around, reversing lines of dialogue—and yet the scene still doesn't quite work. Even making a list has merely resulted in five or ten subtle variations of the same action. It's time to try flipping the action around 180 degrees. Try having one of the characters act

completely out of character. The sweet love interest, for instance, displays a tough side. Or try having the result of an action be the opposite of what currently happens. Instead of the protagonist's act getting them fired, for example, it gets them promoted. Even if this opposing idea isn't ultimately right for your story, it can shake up your thinking and help you see a myriad of new ways into the scene.

3. **The Deletion.** If you've been struggling over a scene or sequence, try dropping it from the script completely. Keep writing. Don't even look at the deleted section for at least one week. You may discover you ultimately didn't need it, or that a better scene or sequence has sprung up to take its place. It may turn out the problem was simply that the scene was in the wrong place, but you weren't able to see this until you removed it. You can also try this technique with dialogue you can't get right or characters who haven't quite gelled: you may find that excising a troublesome line of dialogue makes the rest of the dialogue in the scene stronger, or that removing a character makes the remaining figures more significant and richer.

4. **The Blind Rewrite**. This is a scary one, but it can work wonders. Take what you've written so far. Lock it up in a drawer. Go back to the blank page—and start again. Endlessly rewriting and reworking the words you already have in front of you can cause you to get stuck seeing a scene, character, or plot point only one way. By starting over from scratch, you may discover that the story should really begin later, or that a principal character should enter earlier. You're not trapped by the cause and effect flow of action you've already created. You can view the story anew, and very possibly discover a better way of telling it.

5. **The Stream of Consciousness.** When none of the above tricks work, and you're completely stumped, take a pen and a stack of scrap paper and

write longhand. Write about the character, their background, what they want out of life and out of the story. Write about the setting. Write about the themes you're dealing with in your own life. Write about the themes you feel you want to explore in this screenplay. Write about why you write. Write about why you don't write. Do this for an entire day's writing session if necessary. Similar to how lists work, this technique gives your inner critic a break and lets your subconscious loose. Eventually, you'll break down your internal barriers, because the endless tape loops in your head will have transformed into linear thoughts that end on the page. New ideas will often flood in at this point, and new ways of looking at your character and your plot. You'll discover you've left that roadblock far behind as you race forward with your newfound passion for your story.

THE POWER OF LISTS

The subconscious is the greatest asset a writer has. Unfortunately, by nature, it lies hidden away, beneath the conscious mind. There are many ways to access the subconscious, however, and one of the best is by making lists.

I discussed using lists to come up with new ideas in "How to Find Ideas" in the Before You Begin section. Lists are also a great help after you've come up with the basic idea but nothing has yet been set in concrete. For instance, you can make lists of names for your principal characters and lists of possible professions; lists of locations and of titles for your script. It's also worth making lists of possible plot developments that could result from your set-up. Doing this before you start writing can help you come up with more complex, unpredictable storylines than if you had merely followed your first instinct.

The key to the success of this technique is in making the list mind-numbingly long. In other words, you should attempt to come up with more items for your list than you believe is possible. Say you're looking for an unusual, interesting occupation for your lead. Write the numbers 1 to 50 down the sides of several sheets of paper, and then go. As discussed in the last essay, making the list too long allows your subconscious to spew out everything, without the conscious mind censoring any "dumb ideas." You trick the problem-solving analytical part of your brain into taking a break because you're not committing to anything. You'll get the obvious, clichéd responses out quickly, allowing the more original ideas to come through.

While you're working on the first draft, lists can help you get out of sticky situations and help you overcome blocks. The list doesn't necessarily have to be as long in these cases. If you're having trouble with a patch of dialogue, for instance, try writing it five or six different ways.

Once you have a draft, list-making can help you find the complications you're missing. You can also make lists for how a character might react to a plot point, or of ways to add comedy or background texture to a flat scene. When you're trying to restructure a story, make a list of the scenes you already have, then make a separate list of the scenes you feel you need.

It's literally impossible to list all of the ways lists can help you at *any* stage of development. Lists are one of the easiest and simplest ways to get yourself unstuck, whether you're struggling to come up with a new story or slogging through a difficult rewrite. Lists are quick to do and the surprising results you come up with can renew your enthusiasm for your story.

HOW TO COMMIT

Inevitably in the writing process, there comes a time when you begin to fear the story idea you're working on is not the right story idea for you. Sure, it initially seemed like you and your idea were perfect for each other. But as time goes on, and the hard work begins, doubts creep in. Suddenly, other ideas keep popping into your brain. An overwhelming urge comes over you to abandon your current script and move on to a brighter, better, newer one, certain that *this* idea won't let you down.

The key to writing a good screenplay is not in continually picking up and then dropping ideas in the hopes of finding that unattainable "perfect" film story, but in *committing* to the story you've started and seeing it through to the end. Here are some suggestions on how to accomplish this:

1. <u>Flattery will get you everywhere</u>. Spend an afternoon writing a glowing review of the future movie made from your screenplay. Praise the complex and compelling characters. Note the clever and original plot developments. Compare your screenplay favorably to films you've admired. (You can also do this before you start writing the first draft. Put the review away and pull it out whenever you hit a bad patch—it will remind you of why you loved this idea in the first place.)

2. <u>It's the little things</u>.... Make lists of original, inventive elements you've already come up with for your story—and then think up more: interesting settings; inventive uses of sound, costume, and/or art direction; imaginative character quirks. Type out your favorites lines of dialogue in the current draft and the clever turns of phrase used by the lead characters.

3. <u>Absence makes the heart grow fonder</u>. Don't abandon your screenplay but do take a brief break of a week or two away from it. Distance will give you time to forgive and forget the flaws, so you can remember what initially grabbed you about this idea and made you want to pursue it.

4. <u>Believe in Fate</u>. You came up with this idea for a reason. There was something you were trying to say, some character whose story you felt compelled to tell, some setting or arena you found evocative. Try to remember the moment when your brainstorming clicked and suddenly a full-fledged story idea flew through your head. Bring that passion back to the page.

5. <u>Relationship counseling</u>. Forget about the plot. The easiest way to commit to your story is to fall in love with your characters. If they're distant, superficial figures, your attraction to them won't last, because you won't be emotionally involved. Therefore, get to know them better. Write up character biographies or try one of the exercises from "How to Lure a Character Out of Hiding" in the Characterization section. Study other fictional characters you've loved or people you've known and bring the complexity of those personalities to your characters. Make your characters active in their lives rather than passive observers. It's easier, for the writer as well as the audience, to root for someone who wants something. Write down qualities in your characters that you admire. Figure out what their potential for growth is, and determine what they need to accomplish in order to achieve their dreams. List your characters' flaws as well as their strengths. While their strengths make them heroic, their flaws make them sympathetic. Revisit some of the other essays in the Characterization section for more detailed explorations of these topics.

6. <u>Indulge in a *brief* moment of innocent flirtation</u>. Sometimes the new ideas that keep popping into your head can't be ignored. Although you don't want to become a promiscuous writer with a file cabinet full of brilliant opening sequences that peter out around page 40, it's okay to superficially engage with the idea for a short time. Go ahead and spend an hour with the new idea. Write a quick outline for it. Make a list of the main characters. Jot down a few ideas for scenes. Then put all of these pages in a new folder, put the folder in a drawer (or in a separate section of your computer out of sight of the documents related to your current project), and get back to work. When you've finished the current script you're working on, you'll have one or more new ideas ready to choose from for the next script.

7. **A trial separation.** If, even after writing up an outline for it, one of those other "better" ideas keeps nagging at you, give it a try. The odds are, you'll get hung up around the same page of the script or at the same point in the development process as you did with the project you just abandoned. If this is the case, then the problem isn't your idea but your inability to commit. Return to the previous script and accept that you're going to have to weather the bad days, but have faith that your commitment will make it worth it in the end. Return to the top of this list and try one or more of these techniques again.

8. **Divorce.** However, if you feel more confident and committed to this new idea than you ever did to the previous one, even after problems crop up in the new one, then you probably do need to move on from the first. Perhaps you started the earlier script because you felt it was "commercial" or something you "should" write, but you never really had a deep emotional connection to it. Sometimes a story is ultimately not right for you. You can't change the kind of writer you are to fit a certain type of story. You have to find the story that you are the best writer to tell.

9. <u>Reconciliation</u>. Even if you do end up moving on to a new idea, keep any screenplay beginnings you feel have merit. It may that the story *is* right for you, but you're not in the right place in your life right now to tell it. Five or ten years down the road, when you've grown as a person and as a writer, you might find that the story you once abandoned is now a perfect match.

Sticking with your story, even when the going gets tough, is one of the hardest parts of writing. There will always be rough patches, but often these struggles will bind you more strongly to your story and will help you bring out the depths that were there waiting for you to discover. Don't give up. With every draft you write, you and your story are moving closer to your creative potential.

VIII. <u>BONUS CONTENT</u>

The following essays didn't really fit in the other sections of this book, but I believe they're worth including, because they offer information that can be useful to you as you're working on your script—*and* after it's done. This includes some "behind the scenes" information on what readers do, exactly, and how having this knowledge can make you a more professional writer.

HOW TO GIVE FEEDBACK
WHAT IS COVERAGE?
READER MYTHS & MISCONCEPTIONS
THOUGHTS OF A CONTEST READER

HOW TO GIVE FEEDBACK

In the Revision section, I dealt with how to take feedback—but if you join a critique group or take a writing class, you'll be expected to *give* feedback as well. Here are some useful guidelines in how to be a useful reader to another writer.

1. **<u>Do clarify in advance what kind of notes the writer is looking for</u>**. Do they want just a general overview of what works and what doesn't? Do they want you to focus just on big issues and ignore technical notes, such as typos? Or are they open to any and all notes?

2. **<u>Do tell the writer what works as well as what doesn't</u>**. Not only is praise encouraging, it makes criticism easier to swallow. More importantly, reinforcing the strengths of the script will help the writer keep perspective and not cut something that's working simply because they're too close to it.

3. **<u>Do look for ways to offer certain notes as questions</u>**. If a plot development or character beat isn't clear, don't just say it doesn't work. Ask what the writer was trying to achieve. This can lead to a brief brainstorming session, which can be much more helpful to the writer in finding a way to solve the problem. Along the same lines, point out where there are elements you find interesting that you'd like to know more about.

4. **<u>Don't personalize someone else's story</u>**. If you tend to write hopeful and upbeat stories, and you're asked to comment on a bleak script with a downbeat ending, resist imposing your life view on the writer. Similarly, don't make personal judgments about the writer, such as suggesting they're too cynical. Stick to craft issues related to the script: where does the plot

bog down or become confusing? Are there places where you're unsure of a character's motivation? Is the structure sound? Etc.

5. **<u>Don't rewrite the script for them</u>**. Avoid trying to guide the plot or give suggestions as to how you'd write or rewrite the story. As I've said in other essays, every writer has their own perspectives and experiences, and therefore different writers will execute the same premise differently. Your goal is to help the writer execute their story the best they can.

6. **<u>Don't be offended if the writer rejects some of your comments</u>**. Just as it's up to you to decide what notes are relevant to your script, it's up to your fellow writers to pick and choose what comments they agree with. You may be convinced you're right, but remember, it's your opinion only. If the writer rejects your opinion, it's not a personal slight against you; it's simply a professional choice.

WHAT IS COVERAGE?

Because movie executives receive hundreds of scripts each week, it's not possible for them to read every submission. Instead they rely on a pool of story analysts who write up coverage reports to recommend whether the script is worth being read at the next level. Many agencies and screenwriting contests also rely on readers. An understanding of what coverage is and how it's used can be immensely helpful for writers.

The first page of any coverage report contains general submission information, as well as key story elements such as time period, setting, and genre. However, one of the first things an executive looks at on the cover page is the logline, which is a one-sentence summary of the plot. Executives aren't just looking for originality here. They're looking for dramatic conflict and an active protagonist. For instance, the logline of TOOTSIE might be: "An unemployed actor poses as a woman in order to land a role on a soap opera and gains insight into the female psyche as a result." In one sentence, we know who the character is, what his arc will be, and what the central conflict is.

By the end of your first draft, you should be able to similarly sum up your plot. If you're having trouble doing so, it's probably because you haven't yet figured out the main tension of your story. Before you move on to the next draft of your script, ask yourself: Who is the protagonist? What do they want? What are the obstacles to this goal? The clearer you can be in answering these questions, the stronger not only your logline will be, but your screenplay as well.

Under the logline is a grid that readers use to rate the different elements of a script. The major components are: Premise, Characterization, Plotline, and Dialogue. Some grids also include Structure. Each of these elements is rated as Poor, Fair, Good, or Excellent. It's not the premise that carries the most weight here. While it's important your logline be precise and coherent, it doesn't have to be what's known as "high concept." A mediocre script with an inventive premise is much less likely to be recommended by a reader than a modest premise that's been expertly executed. Companies with a specific mandate may have additional elements on their grid unique to the types of films they make. For instance, Participant Media, which makes socially relevant films has "Social Relevance" listed as one of the elements to be rated.

Finally, the first page includes a recommendation line where the reader gives a script a "Recommend," "Consider," or "Pass." Many coverage reports also include a separate recommendation line for the writing. Therefore, even if the script receives a pass in terms of the story, the reader may still recommend the writer, which can lead to a meeting and possibly writing assignments.

After the cover page is a synopsis of the screenplay, usually one to two pages long. Readers do their best to get across the tone and flavor of the script within this shortened form. However, it helps if the screenplay has a tight plot that develops logically, subplots that are woven in smoothly, and characters who change and grow credibly throughout the script. Screenplays with these qualities make it easier to write engaging synopses.

It can be useful for you to attempt a synopsis yourself. If there are awkward transitions in your summary, you might be missing some key dramatic beats in your plot. If you can drop major events or subplots without changing the overall story, your structure probably needs strengthening. Writing the synopsis makes it easier to pinpoint these types of problems because you're boiling your story down to its essence.

The final page of a coverage report consists of comments. Here a reader analyzes what works and what doesn't work in the screenplay. As with the rating grid on the first page of the report, the elements a reader is likely to focus on in the comments are the characterization and the plot. Characters who are compelling, original, and active tend to be praised. These are characters whom an audience will root for and care about, but, just as importantly, they offer roles that will draw actors. Plots that are inventive, suspenseful, and entertaining will intrigue audiences and also appeal to top directors. (Some coverage reports also include a short paragraph on the cover page summarizing the script's strengths and weaknesses.)

Before you send your screenplay to an agent or producer, first judge it as if you were the reader. Write up a coverage report for it. Be ruthless and honest with yourself. If there are any parts of your script you feel fall short, work on those until you believe they could be rated as "excellent." This will make it much more likely that your screenplay will receive the "recommend" all writers crave.

READER MYTHS & MISCONCEPTIONS

As the so-called "gatekeepers," story analysts are often seen as a malevolent force preventing the writer's work from passing into the more friendly hands of the executive or producer. This is far from true. The following will help you separate fact from fiction.

Myth #1: Readers want or are paid to say "no."

Fact: While executives are expected to champion only those screenplays that are a perfect match for the company's commercial and critical goals, readers are under no such political pressure. Readers are expected to give all good scripts a "recommend" or "consider," because even if the script isn't a good fit for that company, it may still be a worthy writing sample.

Myth #2: If a reader says "no," your script is dead.

Fact: There are plenty of scripts that were bought by the company the script was submitted to despite a "pass" from the reader. This may be because the genre was one the company was looking for; because an actor or other "element" attached appealed to the studio; or because the executive liked the script despite the coverage. Coverage is not a final stamp of approval or disapproval. Coverage is mainly used as a guide for the executive in talking with the agent or producer who submitted the material. It's also a record-keeping device, to help executives keep track of scripts they've received as well as of good writers for future assignments.

Myth #3: Readers only read the first 10 (or 20) pages of a script, and if they don't like it, they stop reading.

Fact: While it's true that producers and executives may only read the beginning of a script, it's the story analyst's job to write a synopsis of the *entire* screenplay. This helps the writer, because we can explain in our comments that while a script has a flawed beginning, we're recommending it because the rest of the story works. A weak start can harm you, but not in the eyes of a reader.

Myth #4: Readers only read the dialogue.

Fact: To be honest, this one has some basis in truth. For romantic comedies, character dramas, and other dialogue-heavy genres, it's possible to get a sense of a story by reading mainly the dialogue. In any genre, long chunks of description are the sign of an amateur writer and will often be skimmed. Sharp, tightly-edited, and well-written description will always be read, however.

Myth #5: Readers are all inexperienced assistants or unpaid interns.

Fact: While assistants and interns often do read scripts as part of their jobs, only at the smallest companies are they the sole readers. All major production companies, producers, and studios employ professional readers, hired because of their skills and experience as story analysts. Many of these professional readers are writers themselves, and most are film school graduates.

Myth #6: Readers are failed writers and resent other writers.

Fact: As mentioned above, it's true that many readers are writers. But this puts them on the side of the writer because they recognize the effort it takes to craft a story well. Because readers aren't the final say on a script purchase, they have nothing to lose and are more likely to take the writer's side and plug a small story or point out a promising talent from an unknown agency.

Myth #7: **Readers are jaded and expect to hate the script before they even start it**.

Fact: Although the majority of scripts that readers cover are "passes," hope still springs eternal in the heart of a story analyst with each new submission. This is partly because the pay for readers is so low that great scripts are the only perk readers get. When a script is well-written and entertaining, reading it is like being paid to watch a good movie.

Myth #8: **Readers steal ideas from the scripts they read**.

Fact: I've never heard of this happening, and this is for a few simple reasons. First of all, readers know the script they're reading is probably being submitted to 20 or 30 other companies, one of which might buy it. Secondly, it would be foolish for a reader to steal an idea for a script they've covered, since the coverage report would present a clear paper trail. Thirdly, as discussed earlier, readers are educated professionals who respect other writers and would never risk both their job as a reader and their career as a writer by setting themselves and the company they work for up for a lawsuit. Finally, a reader learns early on that there are only a limited number of ideas. You may think your idea is original, but chances are there are a half dozen scripts being circulated right now with the same premise. It's the *execution* not the concept that makes or breaks a script.

Myth #9: **Readers are pawns of the studios and only recommend commercial scripts**.

<u>Myth #10</u>: Readers are intellectual snobs and only recommend small, weird, obscure stories.

<u>Fact</u>: Readers only recommend good scripts. A good script has complex characters, an original and compelling plot, and smart, credible dialogue. The screenplay may be a gross-out teen comedy or it may be a thoughtful coming-of-age film. It may be a big-budget science fiction blockbuster or it may be an avant-garde period piece. It doesn't matter. A good script is a good script, and a good script almost always ends up as a movie eventually.

When a screenplay contains any merit, from an inventive concept to lyrical writing, the reader is the first person to champion it. Reading imaginative, entertaining, memorable scripts that they feel would make great films can make a reader's job seem like the best job in the world.

THOUGHTS OF A CONTEST READER

During my long career as a story analyst, I've read for many different screenwriting competitions. One interesting thing I've noticed over the years is that the quality of submissions has improved considerably. Whether this is due to the proliferation of screenwriting software, the availability of screenwriting classes, or the accessibility of produced scripts for study, the screenplays I've read in the last few years are much more professionally crafted and smartly executed than they were when I began reading for contests. The stories also tend to be a lot more inventive and compelling. I see more originality and fewer cookie-cutter genre pieces. There are plenty of thrillers, romantic comedies, and action adventures, etc., but they usually offer an unexpected twist or fresh approach. The characters in all genres have grown more complex and believable, with credible arcs and rich relationships.

While this is good news for readers because it makes their job more enjoyable, it's bad news for writers. Why? Because your competition is a lot fiercer now than it used to be. A great majority of the scripts I read for contests are competently executed. Many are very, very good. A fair number are genuinely outstanding. This makes it necessary for a writer who aims to rise to the top in a contest to write not just a good script, not just a great script, but an *exceptional* one.

So how do you stand out? First of all, make sure you start at the top of the class. No writer can get away with sloppy formatting, dense or inappropriate description, or run-on dialogue. Your characters can't be ordinary and your plot can't be formulaic and predictable. Your premise can't be generic. Beware stories based on a well-known historical person or event, because there are likely to be *at least* two or three other scripts that show up on the same subject. (This occurs more frequently than you'd think.) Scripts based on your own life, though original, can be problematic too. Don't just recount events; make sure you've crafted the experience into a true dramatic narrative. Would the script be as compelling if it were fiction? If the answer is no, then the story doesn't work.

Say you've done it all correctly. Your script is in proper screenplay format, is easy to read, and has complex, compelling characters, an interesting and unique premise, and a smart plot. How do you compete successfully with other authors whose scripts have similar superior qualities?

1. **Make sure the story is developed to its potential**. It's always disappointing to me when a script starts out great, with a fantastic idea, engaging characters, and some good initial twists, and then loses steam and falls apart in the second half. This can be because the relationships weren't adequately developed; because the plot threads weren't successfully unraveled or were tied up in a rushed and contrived manner; because the action got bogged down in repetition; or some combination of all three.

2. **Address the logic issues**. Whether you're writing a bizarre fantasy, a psychological thriller, a broad comedy, or a classic western, you must make the action credible. Research any issues or elements you aren't an expert in. Don't mess with the dates of well-known historical events. Even in a fantasy or sci-fi piece you have to clearly and believably define the rules of the world you've created, and then stay true to them. Logic applies to characterization as well. Don't have a character do something utterly contrary to their personality to suit the plot; if they act unexpectedly, it has to be because you're now revealing another side to them, which then must remain part of their revised characterization for the rest of the script.

3. **<u>Try your best to surprise the reader</u>**. This doesn't mean adding arbitrary plot twists, which will actually frustrate and annoy the reader. Instead, constantly expose deeper levels of your characters; add texture and complexity to the action via unexpected but logical complications. Look for ways to pay off events and elements planted early on. Revise several times. The richer and more detailed you can make your characters and story, the more memorable and surprising your script will be to readers who are used to formulaic plotlines and stock characters.

The fact that there are so many excellent scripts being submitted to contests means that if you don't win, it's not necessarily a reflection of your ability. Keep writing and keep submitting. Even just placing as a quarter or semi-finalist in a contest is a badge of honor because it means you were not only better than the rest, but were among the best of the best.

EPILOGUE

Some of the essays in this book may not apply to the script you're working on now but will apply to future screenplays. Some will be more helpful at different stages in the process of developing whatever script you *are* working on now. As with any book on the craft of writing, take the advice that's useful to you. As I've noted throughout the book, there are exceptions to every rule. It's important to remember, however, that this rule-breaking in successful screenplays is usually the point of the story rather than a by-product of underdevelopment.

The one piece of advice you must follow is: *keep writing*. In the end, you're your own best teacher. As with any skill, from playing tennis to cooking, practice will make you better at it over time. The more you write, the easier it will be to figure out where the problems lie and to solve them.

Happy writing!

FADE OUT.

<u>APPENDIX</u>

IT HAPPENED ONE NIGHT: An Analysis

DIE HARD: An Analysis

RUSHMORE: An Analysis

MOVIES MENTIONED IN THIS BOOK

IT HAPPENED ONE NIGHT
An Analysis

Classic movies from the late 1930s and 1940s are great sources of study for screenwriters. These films almost always follow strict narrative structures with clear delineations (such as fade-outs) between acts and sequences. A good example is IT HAPPENED ONE NIGHT. Although the film was adapted from a short story, screenwriter Robert Riskin expanded and re-structured the plot to fit the standard cinematic form of the time.

<u>ACT ONE</u>

<u>First Sequence</u>: The movie opens by showing a situation in which a conflict exists: Ellie (Claudette Colbert) has married a playboy named King Westley over her father's objections. Her father has imprisoned Ellie on his yacht while he tries to get the marriage annulled. Driven to desperation, Ellie jumps overboard and swims off.

Ellie buys a bus ticket to New York City where King lives. In the same scene, we're introduced to Peter (Clark Gable), who is drunkenly berating his editor over the phone.

Ellie and Peter first meet when Ellie takes Peter's seat on the bus. Soon after, when the bus jerks to a start while Ellie is standing, she falls into Peter's lap. This is the point of attack and also a metaphor for their ensuing relationship: she resents him, yet is forced by circumstances to rely on him.

<u>Second Sequence</u>: The two continue to clash, but their fates are not linked until Peter figures out who Ellie is and then tells his editor he's gotten exclusive rights to her story. (Ellie is unaware of this claim). Both characters' goals have now been established.

ACT TWO

First Sequence: Back on the bus, the "marriage farce" that continues throughout the movie begins when Peter poses as Ellie's husband in order to rescue her from a lascivious passenger named Shapely. When rain washes out the road, the passengers spend the night at an auto camp, and Peter registers himself and Ellie as husband and wife. Peter puts up a blanket separating their beds: "the walls of Jericho." At the end of this scene, Peter offers to help Ellie get to King Westley. Since Peter threatens to call her father if she refuses, Ellie reluctantly agrees. This complication ties them together physically.

Second Sequence: Ellie's father raises the stakes by offering a $10,000 reward for Ellie's capture. Back on the bus, Shapely recognizes Ellie from a news story about the reward. After the driver accidentally drives the bus into a ditch, Shapely takes Peter aside and demands $5000 to keep silent about Ellie. Peter scares Shapely off but realizes he and Ellie are no longer safe riding the bus. This is a key complication in the script. Because of the reward offer, Ellie and Peter have to continue on foot, which makes their journey more difficult. This heightens the dramatic tension while also intensifying the personal relationship.

Third Sequence: During the ensuing scenes, Peter and Ellie's arguments become more personal and they begin to act more like a real couple. They flirt, nearly kiss, and assume traditional roles: Peter forages for food; Ellie treats Peter's wound when he's injured fighting a highway robber. By the end of the sequence, they've achieved intimacy.

Fourth Sequence: Ellie's father announces he's removing his objections to Ellie's marriage. Ellie reads about her father's change of heart in the paper, but she doesn't tell Peter. When they check into a room for the night, Ellie tells Peter that she loves him. He rejects her and she's crushed. Later, Peter sneaks out. He delivers his story to his editor in order to get $1000, so he can propose to Ellie. Believing Peter has abandoned her, Ellie calls her father. As Peter drives back to the motel, he spots Ellie driving off the other way in King Westley's arms. Both characters are now at their lowest points.

ACT THREE

First Sequence: Ellie confesses to her father that she's in love with Peter. Peter later visits Ellie's father and asks for repayment of his expenses. He shows no interest in the $10,000 reward, and he confesses that he loves Ellie. By taking these actions, Peter and Ellie set into motion the possibility for a happy ending.

Second Sequence: As Ellie's father walks Ellie down the aisle, he tells her about his conversation with Peter. At the altar, Ellie turns and flees, echoing the opening scene of the film. In the final scene, Ellie and Peter check into a motel, where they let the "walls of Jericho" fall.

The success of this film, like any film, is not due simply to a tight structure, but also to rich characters and inspired moments in the action. IT HAPPENED ONE NIGHT contains many iconic film moments, from the bus passengers' singing of "The Man on the Flying Trapeze," to the "walls of Jericho" conceit, to the hitch-hiking scene. What the structure does is help create the illusion that the action is unfolding according to an inevitable sense of cause and effect, instead of coming across as a random collection of quirky beats.

DIE HARD
An Analysis

Mainstream commercial fare, such as action films, are also great to study for structure. Here's the breakdown of one of the most critically and commercially successful films in the action genre.

ACT ONE

First Sequence: The film opens with New York cop John McCain (Bruce Willis) flying to L.A. to spend Christmas with his estranged wife Holly (Bonnie Bedelia). As the story begins, a problem already exists: John and Holly are on the verge of divorce. He arrives at her office Christmas party, they spar, and she leaves him to join her colleagues.

Second Sequence: Terrorists break into the building and kill the desk guard. We meet the terrorist leader, the dapper and debonair Hans Gruber (Alan Rickman). Hans and his men burst into the party and open fire, then take the employees hostage. (This is the point of attack.) Meanwhile, in another office, John hears the bullets and remains hidden.

ACT TWO

First Sequence: Gruber orders Takagi, the CEO, to turn over the $640 million in bonds located in the company vault. Takagi insists it's impossible to open the vault, which has seven locks, including an electromagnetic one. Angry at Takagi's refusal to cooperate, Gruber kills him. After John sets off the fire alarm, and then kills a terrorist who comes after him, Gruber realizes there's a man on the loose in the building. Holly guesses it's John. John takes the dead terrorist's walkie-talkie to the roof and calls out a "May

Day." The cops are wary but send a patrol car, driven by a cop named AL, for a routine check.

Second Sequence: While John plays cat and mouse with the terrorists, Al chats with a terrorist posing as the desk guard. Convinced all is well, Al drives off. Desperate, John breaks a window and throws out one of the dead terrorists. This finally gets the attention of the cops. Squad cars surround the building—but Gruber is unfazed; this is part of his plan.

Third Sequence: Al picks up John on the walkie-talkie, but John won't tell Al who he is, because he doesn't want Gruber to know. Police chief Robinson concludes John is a terrorist and is working alone, despite Al's instincts to the contrary. Robinson insists on sending men inside, even though John warns they'll be slaughtered. As expected, the terrorists shoot at the cops.

Fourth Sequence: Gruber learns from another employee that John is a cop. Outside, the FBI arrives and takes over. As John continues his battle inside, the feds cut the power, allowing the terrorists to get through the last lock on the vault. John fears all is lost and asks Al to tell Holly he's sorry for his behavior.

ACT THREE

First Sequence: Gruber learns Holly is John's wife, from a TV news report. John finds the missiles Gruber has brought in and calls Al to warn him. When police helicopters land on the roof, John fires at them, having realized the roof is wired to explode. The cops fire back. Gruber blows up the roof and John grabs a firehouse and dives off, then re-enters through a window. John finds Gruber, who has taken Holly hostage. John tricks Gruber and then shoots him. Gruber falls out the window to his death.

Second Sequence: John and Holly emerge from the building. John and Al hug, having bonded through the ordeal, just as the last surviving terrorist appears. Al kills him and saves the day.

This film works well for many reasons. First of all, every sequence contains a complication that makes John's situation worse and raises the stakes. John also has a clear arc in the story. He begins both physically and mentally vulnerable (he's barefoot, and he's initially at a loss as to how to fight the terrorists), but during the course of the story, his wits sharpen and his relationship with Al over the walkie-talkie builds his confidence. John's attitude towards Holly changes as well, giving him an emotional arc.

By having the terrorists speak in German, with no subtitles, we're able to watch their actions without getting bogged down in exposition. We know what they're saying from what they're *doing*. Another plus is that all of John's actions are logical and smart. Unlike films where the protagonist makes foolish choices that inevitably go wrong, or carries out implausible superhuman tasks, John acts believably yet wisely. For example, he runs to the roof and calls for help on the walkie-talkie, which is something we might have done in his place. When this action fails, it is genuinely upsetting and creates real suspense.

The best action movies, the ones that become classics, contain many of these same qualities—qualities all writers should aim for in their screenplays.

RUSHMORE
An Analysis

While it's usually easy to detect the structure of an older movie, or of a straight genre movie, independent films often appear more fluid and extemporaneous, free from the bounds of a narrative framework. However, while the sequences might not each take place all in one location or on one day, or be set-off by fades or dissolves, seemingly free-form modern films with their loose narratives still contain an inner structure, and they build dramatically in much the same way as their forerunners. Take RUSHMORE, written by Wes Anderson and Owen Wilson, for instance.

ACT ONE

First Sequence: The movie opens, showing a situation in which a problem exists: Max Fisher (Jason Schwartzman) is so caught up in extracurricular activities at his beloved private school, Rushmore, that he's on the verge of flunking out. Max meets Mr. Blume (Bill Murray), whose sons attend the school, and Max and Blume click as kindred spirits. Meanwhile, Max's single-minded devotion to Rushmore begins to change when he sets eyes on Miss Cross (Olivia Williams), the pretty first grade teacher. This is the point of attack.

Second Sequence: In an attempt to win Miss Cross's affections, Max first campaigns to bring back Latin, and then convinces Blume to fund a school aquarium in her honor. At the end of this sequence, Max hits a low point when he declares his love to Miss Cross while out to dinner with her, her boyfriend, and Blume, Miss Cross rejects him. However, he has not given up on his goal, and now Blume and Miss Cross are aware of it. The major conflict of the story has begun.

ACT TWO

First Sequence: Max, still believing he has a chance with Miss Cross, moves forward with the aquarium, but Miss Cross doesn't show up for the groundbreaking. The school headmaster is furious when he finds out about the aquarium plan and expels Max. Now Max has not only lost Miss Cross, but he's lost Rushmore as well.

Second Sequence: Max manages to patch things up with Miss Cross by inserting Blume into the mix as a sort of chaperon/cheerleader. However, Max remains naïve about his situation and the world at large. He snubs Margaret, a student at his new school who attempts to befriend him, and he's oblivious to the growing attraction between Miss Cross and Blume. Finally, Max learns Blume has been seeing Miss Cross secretly and is devastated.

Third Sequence: Max declares war on Blume. The rivalry between the two quickly escalates, culminating in Max's arrest. Learning that Miss Cross has resigned from Rushmore, Max shows up on her last day at school and makes a pass at her. She chews him out, forcing him to face how ignorant he really is about life. Max meets with Blume and admits defeat in their battle over Miss Cross.

Fourth Sequence: Max drops out of school and goes to work in his father's barbershop. He runs into Blume, who sadly reports he's no longer seeing Miss Cross. With Blume out of the way, Max tricks Miss Cross into letting him into her house and then tries to kiss her, but she rejects him once again. It finally becomes clear to Max, that he will never have Miss Cross.

ACT THREE

First Sequence: Max finally accepts the loss of Rushmore, Miss Cross, and Blume. He's changed now, matured. He decides to return to public school and embrace his life there. He reconciles with Blume and encourages him to go after Miss Cross. Blume revives the aquarium idea but once again, Miss Cross is a no-show at the opening ceremonies.

Second Sequence: Max invites Miss Cross and Blume to his new play at the public school and arranges for them to sit together. The play is a huge success; Blume and Miss Cross tentatively reconcile; Max embarks on a romance with Margaret.

RUSHMORE demonstrates its conscious attention to structure by using title cards to set off the first and third sequences of the second act, as well as the second sequence of the third act. The script also deftly weaves together dozens of subplots, such as Max's friendship with his Rushmore classmate Dirk and Max's war with a bully named Duncan. Each of these minor throughlines contain clear beginnings, middles, and ends, as well as complications, crises, and climaxes similar to those of the main story. This complex but meticulously crafted structure results in a film in which the tension consistently builds, making it involving from beginning to end.

MOVIES MENTIONED IN THIS BOOK

127 HOURS

AND THEN THERE WERE NONE (1945)

THE APARTMENT

BAD NEWS BEARS

BEFORE SUNRISE

THE BIG EASY

BLADE RUNNER

BRIDGE ON THE RIVER KWAI

CAPE FEAR (1962)

CASABLANCA

CHARADE

CHINATOWN

CLUELESS

THE CRYING GAME

THE DEVIL WORE PRADA

DIE HARD

DOUBLE INDEMNITY

EIGHTH GRADE

ELF

THE ETERNAL SUNSHINE OF THE SPOTLESS MIND

GET OUT

GONE WITH THE WIND

GOSFORD PARK

THE GRADUATE

IT HAPPENED ONE NIGHT

L.A. CONFIDENTIAL

THE LADY EVE

LAURA

LES DIABOLIQUES

LETHAL WEAPON

LOVE AFFAIR (1939)

THE MANCHURIAN CANDIDATE (1962)

THE MASK

MEET THE PARENTS

MEMENTO

ON THE WATERFRONT

THE PRINCESS BRIDE

PSYCHO (1960)

RAIDERS OF THE LOST ARK

RUSHMORE

SCHINDLER'S LIST

SCHOOL OF ROCK

SHAKESPEARE IN LOVE

THE SHAPE OF WATER

A SIMPLE PLAN

THE SIXTH SENSE

SLEUTH (1972)

SOME LIKE IT HOT

STAR WARS

THE STING

TOOTSIE

THE USUAL SUSPECTS

WHAT WE DO IN THE SHADOWS

WITNESS

THE WIZARD OF OZ

WORKING GIRL

RESOURCES

BOOKS ON CRAFT

SCREENWRITING CONTESTS

ONLINE RESOURCES

BOOKS ON CRAFT

This is far from a comprehensive list. The first two books are good introductions to screenwriting and the remainder are books I consult often, but there are dozens of other worthy screenwriting and fiction writing books out there, including others by the authors of these books. I've read many, many more that I didn't list, and I've always learned *something* from them. While I'd caution against spending too much time reading craft books at the expense of your writing time, it's good to have a couple of guides to refer to when you're starting out and, later, when you're stuck. A craft book you haven't yet read might also offer you a fresh perspective on an issue you've been struggling with, by presenting an approach that finally allows you to break through a block.

Screenplay by Syd Field

This was the first screenwriting book I was exposed to, because it was the assigned reading when I was in film school. At that time, it was *the* book on screenwriting, and the one that preceded most of the rest. Much of it feels dated now, but it works as a basic overview of script structure and is therefore a good introduction to the craft.

How to Make a Good Script Great by Linda Seger

Another early entry in the field, written by a well-known script doctor who began her career, like I did, as a reader. Writing coverage of hundreds of scripts, and having to clearly explain what's working or not and why, makes for a great education in how to identify problems and fix them, which is what Seger does in this book. A sequel, *Creating Unforgettable Characters*, is also helpful for problems related to characterization.

How to Write a Script in 21 Days by Viki King

I love this book. I don't believe you can actually write a script this fast (complete with revision and polish!), but this book has one of the clearest and most accessible explanations of film structure I've found. The book includes detailed chapters on creating a basic outline, on writing a fast first draft, and on what to look for when revising that draft.

Wired for Story by Lisa Cron

This was the assigned text in a university screenwriting class I taught and I'm happy to have been introduced to it. This book digs even more deeply into character than the Seger sequel referenced above, concentrating on the psychology of characters and how what drives them propels a story. Although the book is ostensibly for fiction writers, it often references movies as examples and it works just as well if not better for scripts. I've learned a lot from it.

Save the Cat Strikes Again by Blake Snyder

Snyder's first book, *Save the Cat*, sported the subtitle: "The Last Book on Screenwriting You'll Ever Need." He then, ironically, went on to write two more. The first book was introduced to me by a fellow novelist and I used it while writing the sequel to my first YA novel. I now own all three of Snyder's books, but if you only read one, *this* is the one to buy. It restates much of the information introduced in the first book and then goes into greater depth on these concepts, such as how to break down the beats of your plot before you begin your first draft. I've found the book particularly useful for its discussion of the midpoint, as well as of the third act finale. It's worth noting that Snyder's lingo is often used by Hollywood development executives, so the book is worth reading for that alone.

20 Master Plots (and How to Build Them) by Ronald B. Tobias
I refer to this book regularly, for both novels and scripts, when I'm just beginning to flesh out an idea. The book lists basic plot concepts, such as "Quest," "Rivalry," and "Forbidden Love," and then breaks them down into three dramatic "phases" (essentially the three acts). The book also discusses various properties each concept generally needs and gives examples, usually from classic literature.

The Modern Library Writer's Workshop by Stephen Koch
I can't remember where I found this book, but I've reread it at least a half-dozen times. It's a guidebook of sorts and aimed at novelists, but it's essentially a source for inspiration and encouragement, applicable to writers of all forms. Koch distills previously published advice from famous writers, such as Ray Bradbury and Kurt Vonnegut, covering everything from "how to begin" to the final polish. He also adds tips based on his own experiences teaching fiction.

The Hidden Tools of Comedy by Steve Kaplan
The Comic Toolbox by John Vorhaus
These are for the comedy writers out there. Each of these was referred to me by a different writer friend, and I've found them both useful. The first focuses mainly on character and how that drives the best comedies. The second covers a wide variety of humor elements.

SCREENWRITING CONTESTS

Because there are so many screenplay competitions, and because new ones appear all the time, it's impossible to include an up-to-date list in a book. Therefore, I've listed only two of the best known contests, to get you started. The descriptions below were current as of this writing, but check the competition's websites for any changes, as well as for information on qualifications and deadlines.

The Nicholl Fellowship (oscars.org/nicholl): Offered through the Academy of Motion Picture Arts & Sciences, this is the gold medal of screenwriting competitions. Five winners are given a large stipend to help support them over the following year while they work on their next script, assisted by their mentor: a professional screenwriter matched specifically with them. The Nicholl does a great job of publicizing the scripts by all top 10 finalists, and these scripts are often solicited and read by the major studios and film companies. Even placing as a semi-finalist or quarter-finalist is considered a badge of honor and will often help a writer land an agent or manager, and/or get their script read.

The Austin Film Festival Screenplay & Teleplay Competition (austinfilmfestival.com): This competition is held as part of the Austin Film Festival and currently offers several categories for prizes, including comedy feature, drama feature, TV pilot, best short screenplay, and fiction podcast—among others. As with the Nicholl, being a finalist is often enough of a validation to land a writer an agent.

See **Film Freeway** in "Online Resources" on the next page to find other contests you may qualify for based on your background and what form or genre you're writing in.

ONLINE RESOURCES

As with books on craft, this list comprises only a few of the many, many good screenwriting-related sites out there.

Film Freeway (filmfreeway.com): A great searchable database of film and screenwriting competitions. Search via a number of factors. For example, there are diversity-driven contests for underrepresented writers, contests focused solely on female writers, and competitions for writers who are specifically interested in working on TV series—to name a few. Film commissions often hold competitions for stories set in their states or regions.

Save the Cat (savethecat.com): An accompaniment to Blake Snyder's books, run by a group of STC loyalists. The website offers a lot of useful advice, including dozens of "beat sheets" submitted by followers, in which they break down the structures of well-known films (as well as some TV shows and a few novels) into the elements and sequences Snyder outlines in his books. For brainstorming ideas, there is a list of ten exercises for coming up with horror plots, and ten for comedies.

Script Notes (johnaugust.com/scriptnotes): One of the first and possibly one of the best known screenwriting blogs. Screenwriter and novelist John August also hosts a Script Notes podcast covering the material on the blog.

Writer's Guild of America (wga.org): There is a wealth of information here, even if you're not yet in the guild, including a link to register your script before you send it out.

Writer's Guild Foundation Library (wgfoundation.org/library/visit-us): If you live in or are visiting Los Angeles, make a plan to visit the library, which is open to the public. It contains thousands of professional scripts that anyone can look at as samples, either in print or via iPads that the library staff will loan to you while you're at the library. In some cases, there are multiple drafts of well-known features and complete collections of scripts for all the episodes from a TV series. The library also has several TV show bibles (which contain the original pitch for the show as well as lists of potential episodes).

Word Player (wordplayer.com): Another one of the first screenwriting blogs, created by Terry Rossio and Ted Elliott, the writers of the original PI-RATES OF THE CARIBBEAN. The columns stopped a few years ago, but the forum is still active and there's a wealth of information in the archives.

ACKNOWLEDGEMENTS

Thank you to Joanne Lammers, without whom Script Nannies wouldn't have existed and the Script Buzz column never would have been written. A round of thanks must also go to the Script Buzz subscribers and Script Nannies clients, whose interest in the columns kept me writing them over several years, prompting me to find new topics and problems to tackle—which inevitably helped my own writing.

Thanks to Rebecca Lesner Schlaeger, Max Schwartz, and Marty Stevens-Heebner for nagging me to collect my columns into an e-book. I finally did it!

(Extra thanks to Rebecca for moral and technical support.)

Lastly, thank you to Jesse Gordon for helping me format the book for publication.

"How to Develop Your Premise into a Compelling Plot" was previously published on www.writing-world.com.

"What is Coverage?" appeared in a longer form on www.writing-world.com.

"Reader Myths & Misconceptions" appeared in a longer form on www. scriptmag.com.

ABOUT THE AUTHOR

Kathy McCullough is a screenwriter and novelist who spent over 20 years as a Hollywood story analyst, both full- and part-time. She's written scripts for the Disney Channel, Hallmark, and Lifetime, among other companies. Her YA novels *Don't Expect Magic* and its sequel *Who Needs Magic?* were published by Random House/Delacorte Press. She's also written children's books for Disney Worldwide Publishing and Houghton Mifflin. You can find out more about her and her writing projects at www.kathymccullough books.com.

Made in the USA
Las Vegas, NV
31 May 2021